Ephesians 5:11

3-23-2007

In God
We ~~Trust~~ Betrayed

Peter S. Grasso Jr
July 30, 2006

Table of Contents

Special Thanks

Amazing Grace, how sweet the sound, that saved a wretch like me. I once was lost and now I'm found, was blind but now I see.

John Newton

Writing this book is definitely out of my comfort zone. I am neither a very good writer nor speaker. Therefore, I give praise and thanks to the Holy Spirit, whose still, small voice has been a source of strength and encouragement to this rebellious servant.

I also thank my beautiful wife, Debbie, for her commitment to our marriage when most would have thrown in the towel a long time ago. Debbie is a "doer of the word" and continues to be a role model and the primary source of tremendous strength in my life.

I would like to thank Pastor David Moore from "Moore on Life Ministries" for influencing my heart during his radio ministry when I was at my lowest point in life and for his teachings and continuous support; and Pastor Greg Jennings from New Life Christian Church, who made himself available to me when I was searching for a way to be right with the Lord. I would also like to convey a very special thanks to Minister Joe Wright for his courage to deliver a truthful and powerful message during the Kansas Senate opening prayer in 1996. Minister Wright was the spark within my heart and my primary inspiration for writing this book.

Lastly, I want to thank my mom and dad for their continuing prayers and their faith and encouragement. They never gave up on me. Their persistent prayers kept my heavenly Father scanning the horizon for this prodigal son's return.

It is my hope that this book will serve as a wakeup call to those who know God, but have been drifting along this sea called life without really making a difference for the kingdom of God. To those who do not have a personal relationship with the Lord, it is my deepest desire that this book will inspire you to connect with your maker.

Jesus is coming back soon... Now is the time to make a difference before it is too late for this country.

A Call to
All People of Faith

The content of this book is derived from readings and personal studies of the Bible in combination with the cultural history of the United States. As I began to study the nation of Israel in the Old Testament, there were significant parallels to our situation, and "red flags" were raised to which the people of this great nation should give careful attention. We are not so isolated from the world nor so powerful that we cannot be defeated and destroyed as a nation and dispersed as a people.

Whether you are a Catholic, Baptist, Methodist, Presbyterian, Lutheran, Evangelical, or someone just curious about Christianity, I highly encourage you to blow the dust off the family Bible and look up the references within this book. You owe it to yourself to seek the truth, which has been hidden and obscured by a vocal minority within this country. We are not well on this planet, and the future is going to get a whole lot worse before the second coming of Jesus Christ. Each generation is getting more corrupt, more immoral, and more wicked than the previous generation—just as the nation of Israel was during the Old Testament times in the readings of 1st Kings, 2nd Kings, 1st Chronicles, and 2nd Chronicles.

There are many books on shelves today that focus on biblical teachings. Some focus on the love of God, which is great and provides plenty of information about how to live a life that is pleasing to God. The study of Jesus alone is a teaching of ultimate love, sacrifice, forgiveness, and redemption. I highly encourage you to ground yourself with these readings to expand upon your personal walk with your Lord and Savior. However, it is critical that we recognize the warning of impending ruin that is facing this country if we do nothing. It is important that you also understand God's provision for you and your family during these end times.

This book gets to the point in a manner that most people and many preachers are afraid to address head-on. We are a nation that is heavily backsliding ever since the 1947 Supreme Court ruling that created the separation of church and state. The American Civil Liberties Union (ACLU) and the secular humanist crowd have used that ruling as a battle cry in their attacks to undermine the moral fabric that is the foundation of this country's cultural and moral norms. Today, we are a people who have abandoned our Lord and protector, a society that is systematically throwing God out of all aspects of our lives and communities, and a country that is on the brink of receiving God's exacting judgment. The battle lines have already been drawn. Israel went into captivity and was scattered across the globe due to the iniquity of its people and their abandonment of God.

> And the nations shall know that the house of Israel **went into captivity for their iniquity,** because they dealt so treacherously with me that **I hid my face from them** and **gave them into the hand of their adversaries, and they all fell by the sword. I dealt with them according to their uncleanness and**

their transgressions, and hid my face from them.

Ezekiel 39:23-24 (NIV)

If this country continues to head down the path of moral degradation, we will lose God's divine protection and guarantee our own destruction as God's judgment is exacted against the leaders and doers of iniquity. You are part of this battle, whether you like it or not. You can stand idly by and watch it unfold before you as the faithful continue to be ostracized by our political and legal system, or you can take a stand to turn events around.

Remember that within this great nation, we, the people of faith, still outnumber our adversaries, who are comprised of every group, agency, government, and person who is determined to take our religious freedom from us. Sin always has a consequence. The United States of America is not above God's judgment. You can and must make a difference, for the fight at hand is greater than any action a terrorist can muster. The stakes are infinitely and eternally higher.

Our Country Is
Spiraling Out of Control

Over the past 230 years, the United States of America has transitioned from a country founded on the principles of Christianity to that of a secular humanistic society that has turned its back on God under the guise of constitutionally guaranteed freedoms. The ACLU has been the catalyst for the steady derogation of our country's culture over the past eighty years. Today:

- Our children are being brainwashed in schools and colleges, where God is forbidden. It is part of the secular humanist's agenda to influence our next generation into conformance to a liberal mindset, alienated from the godly principles that have made our country great in the past.
- Many of our leaders are corrupt and self-serving, or "political party-serving" rather than serving the people by whom they have been elected. This applies to both Democrats and Republicans alike.
- The founding principles of our constitution are being ignored or changed by liberal judges. This is being leveraged strategically by the ACLU,

which has aligned its agenda with these judges to fashion the law in its favor. In most cases, this is being achieved against the will of the people, while spineless politicians sit idly by instead of defending the constitution to which they have sworn their allegiance.

- Our culture and society are being torn apart by large, well-funded associations, political action groups, the liberal news media, and more recently, by some major corporations.
- Christians are being confined to the churches for fear of losing their not-for-profit status, while great iniquities and filth are being broadcast to the masses under the protection of "freedom of speech."
- The very fabric of our Judeo-Christian society is being torn apart by a cancer within the churches that is more willing to compromise God's moral standard than to take a stand against the prevailing winds of secular humanism, liberalism, and indifference.
- Those who take a moral stand are considered out of touch, right-wing zealots, while everything else is vigorously defended in the name of tolerance.

As a result of our disobedience to God's moral principles, this nation is on a road parallel to the road taken by the nation of Israel when it abandoned its true love for God and followed after its own wickedness. In the end, that road led to the destruction of Israel and to its people being scattered for thousands of years. There is evidence today that the United States is being systematically pulled apart as a result of a judgment that is being exacted by a righteous God. The warning signs are obvious.

Because you did not serve the LORD your God
with joyfulness and gladness of heart, by reason of the
abundance of all things, [48] therefore you shall serve
your enemies whom the LORD will send against
you, in hunger and thirst, in nakedness, and in want
of all things; and he will put a yoke of iron upon your
neck, until he has destroyed you. [49] The LORD will
bring a nation against you from afar, from the end of
the earth, as swift as the eagle flies, a nation whose
language you do not understand, [50] a nation of stern
countenance, who shall not regard the person of the
old or show favor to the young...

Deuteronomy 28:47-50 (NIV)

The Lord will not be mocked... Whatever one sows, one
shall reap—and that is most definitely true for our nation
as well (Galatians 6:9). One only needs to read 1st Kings,
2nd Kings, 1st Chronicles, and 2nd Chronicles in the Bible to
see how the majority of Israel's leaders abandoned the Lord
to seek after their own self-interests. With each evil ruler,
the people fell deeper and deeper into iniquity, sin, and the
abandonment of God's principles. Finally, during the
reign of King Manasseh, the children of Israel strayed so far
from the governing principles of their Lord that there was no
distinction between the children of Israel and their enemies
from whom the Lord delivered them.

> Because Manasseh, King of Judah, has
> committed these abominations, and has done
> things more wicked than all that the Amorites
> did, who were before him, and has made Judah
> also to sin with his idols; therefore thus says
> the LORD, the God of Israel, Behold, I am
> bringing upon Jerusalem and Judah such evil
> that the ears of every one who hears of it will

tingle. **And I will stretch over Jerusalem the measuring line of Samaria, and the plummet of the house of Ahab; and I will wipe Jerusalem as one wipes a dish, wiping it and turning it upside down.**

2 Kings 21:11-13 (NIV)

King Manasseh so thoroughly corrupted Israel that the Lord raised up King Nebuchadnezzar of the Babylonians (modern-day Iraq) to systematically destroy Israel (2 Kings Chapter 24 and 25). Over time, Israel was reduced to ruins, its people removed from their homeland, with a remnant of the survivors scattered throughout the world. Israel remained a scattered nation for thousands of years until finally it returned to power in 1947. This occurred after a great holocaust, which was predicted in the Old Testament by the profit Ezekiel thousands of years ago (Ezekiel 37:1-14 and 21-22).

Likewise, if the United States of America and its people do not change course from that of an amoral nation to a moral one, we will most certainly be on a parallel course toward God's judgment. Yet before we can change this country and the world, we need to evaluate our own relationship with God on an individual basis.

My first question to you is simple: How are you connecting with God? This is a very important question that only you can answer. If you are not connecting with God and do not wish to, then the remaining chapters within this book will come across as just nonsensical ramblings from another Christian zealot. If you are connecting with God or desire to connect with Him, then please read on.

We All
Need a Savior

And just as it is appointed for men to die
once, and after that comes judgment...
Hebrews 9:27 (NIV)

The United States is not immune to the Lord's justice. The Hebrew nation was God's chosen people. Yet God exacted His judgment on that nation by leading them into captivity by their enemies when they turned their back on Him. Having acted as God did with Israel, His chosen people, how long do we expect Him to tolerate the great abominations occurring within this country? As you read this, you might believe that our Lord is a God of love and that He would never exact His judgment upon this country. Or would He?

In the end times, which I firmly believe we are in, the Book of Revelation is clear that a large portion of the world's population will be destroyed due to its wickedness. We currently have a world population of more than 6.4 billion people. If this prediction is true, more than one-third of the world's population will be destroyed by fire. Billions will die due to God's judgment.[a] Is this possible? Would God destroy so many people to exact His righteous judgment?

Why do people think that mankind is worthy of favor from God anyway? Who are we to consider ourselves significant, particularly if our merits are viewed from a universal perspective? Nevertheless, most people think in terms of relative goodness as compared to God's standard of perfection, which is in absolutes. Our God is a God of love, but He is also an exactor of judgment as a penalty for sin. That is God's nature, which we cannot change or compromise, irrespective of what some of the "churches" within this country are teaching their members.

The bottom line is that we are either all good or all bad in our feeble efforts to win God's favor according to our own merits. If you can live a life that adheres to the hundreds of laws within the Old Testament without wavering in both thought and action, then you can earn your way to heaven. However, there has never been a person in existence that has upheld that standard—except Jesus. Therefore, we are all bad to some degree. Without a savior, we cannot make it to heaven according our reasoning or feeble attempts toward righteousness. There is no gray area here. It is a pass/fail grade only. God does not rate on a bell curve, where passing is a score of sixty percent or above. Neither does God compare your good works to your sins to calculate a positive or negative result.

To further put a damper on those who think that they have lived a good life and are worthy of entrance to heaven, the Bible states:

> ...For **ALL** have sinned, and come short of the glory of God.
>> Romans 3:23 (NIV)

> For this [cause], even as by one man sin entered into the world [Adam], and by sin

death; and thus death passed upon all men, for that **ALL** have sinned.

Romans 5:12 (NIV)

For the **wages of sin is death,** but the free gift of God is eternal life in Christ Jesus our Lord.

Romans 6:23 (NIV)

The bottom line is that we have all come up short. I would like to take a moment to demonstrate the way God sees it from the following illustration of five dead bodies.

The Five Dead Bodies

Imagine five dead bodies lying face-up on the ground. The first is freshly dead and appears like someone resting comfortably with his arms across his chest. The fifth person has been dead for a few years, thus the body is badly decomposed, rotten to the core with only skeletal remains. The other three bodies are in different degrees of decay, from the freshly dead person to the one at the end who is rotten to the core.

The common factor among all five bodies in this illustration is that they are all dead. Irrespective of the appearance of the person that is freshly dead, he, too, is dead.

The bottom is line is that we are all spiritually dead and separated from God as the result of the first sin that was committed in this world—Adam and Eve's disobedience. Regardless of how good we are in our lives, how well we treat our families, or how generous we are to others, we are all spiritually dead, for "ALL have sinned…" according to God in Romans 5:12.

Going back to the illustration, you could have been living a very sinful life and alienating yourself from God. You might be saying to yourself: "I'm the one that is rotten to the core, who's been dead for many years." Despite your failures, disappointments, and repeated shortcomings, you have something in common with the first freshly dead body—you, too, are dead.

If you are grasping at what the Bible is telling you, mankind has a serious problem. There is not a man, woman, or child on this earth that can earn their way to heaven. That is the reality, irrespective of how hard you try. And if you think you can, guess what?

> But, we are **all** as an unclean thing, and **all our righteousness** are as filthy rags; and **we all** do fade as a leaf; and our iniquities, like the wind, have taken us away.
> Isaiah 64:6 (NIV)

Even our good deeds just don't measure up to God's standard. The Bible says that Jesus was sent to this earth to reconcile us with God. He was the ultimate sacrificial lamb that was slaughtered on the cross for mankind. He died for us. He did not have to. He chose to die in our place, for He knew that we could not save ourselves. And furthermore, He knew that we would continuously fail in this thing called life.

> Then as one man's trespass (Adam) **led to condemnation for all men**, so **one man's act of righteousness leads to acquittal** and life for all men.
> Romans 5:18 (NIV)

We did not earn God's favor, nor did we deserve it. It is a fact that God loves us just the way we are, and He created a provision for our spiritual wellbeing through the sacrifice of Jesus on the cross. We come into a relationship and stand with

God not through our actions, but by Jesus' blood covering our sins.

> But, God shows his love for us in that, while
> we were yet sinners, Christ died for us.
> Romans 5:8 (NIV)

Think about the price God paid on our behalf. When I was a program manager for a large government account, my job required that I travel a lot. I have always found it amazing how insignificant mankind is from a thirty thousand-foot viewpoint, peering out the window of an aircraft at night. The glow of city lights is the only visible clue to mankind's presence below. Looking up, you see the mass of stars in the sky.

Scientists estimate that the stars in the universe number more than 10^{22} (10 followed by 22 zeros), and that estimate does not include planets. Yet within this universal oasis, we are singled out as being loved enough by God, the Creator of the universe, that He would sacrifice his only begotten Son as a payment for our sins. He did this to have a relationship with us and to redeem our souls.

> For God so loved the world that **he gave**
> his only Son, that whoever believes in Him
> should not perish, but have eternal life.
> John 3:16 (NIV)

This is the part that everyone knows from football sporting events, with those crazy Christians waving "John 3:16" signs in the end zone. However, as you continue reading the passage, you come to understand that a decision and action is required on behalf of the message's recipient.

For God sent the Son into the world, not to
condemn the world, but that the world might
be saved through him. He who believes in
Him is not condemned; he who does not
believe is condemned already, because he has
not believed in the name of the only Son of
God. And this is the judgment, that the light
has come into the world, and men loved darkness rather than light, because their deeds
were evil. **For every one who does evil hates
the light, and does not come to the light,
lest his deeds should be exposed**.

John 3:17-20 (NIV)

God's sacrifice for your sins came at a high cost. Many
read John 3:16 and say to themselves "thank You, God," then
move on as if it were just a nice-to-know message of encouragement. Yet the people of this world are doing evil in the
eyes of God, especially within this country. There are many
in positions of authority and leadership that "love darkness
rather than the light." There is a whole secular humanistic
movement that is corrupting our youth into a mindset that
what is right for you is what matters. The leaders of this nation
have collectively pushed God to the side and, in some cases,
denied our children access to their Creator's teachings.

The Bible states that "**Every one who does evil hates
the light and does not come to the light**." That light is
Jesus, the Son of God.

It is becoming more obvious each day that there are forces
within our country that hate the light. These forces are hell-
bent on denying God's influence within our government and
educational system. Furthermore, these forces are removing
the symbols and references of God within our country. They
are also teaching a politically correct version of our history
to our children as being void of God, which is an inaccurate

portrayal of our country's true background. And they are on the attack of anyone who professes their faith in a public forum as being "offensive" and "inappropriate." It is incredibly ironic that tolerance is preached everywhere, except when it comes to believers of God.

My question to you is where do you stand in all of this? If all have sinned and have fallen short of the glory of God, and if all our righteousness is but a filthy rag, is it no wonder that so many love the darkness and not the light?

> While we were still weak, at the right time Christ died for the ungodly. Why, one will hardly die for a righteous man—though perhaps for a good man one will dare even to die. But God shows his love for us in that, while we were yet sinners, Christ died for us.
>
> Romans 5:6-8 (NIV)

> Again, Jesus spoke to them, saying, "I am the light of the world; he who follows me will not walk in darkness, but will have the light of life."
>
> John 8:12 (NIV)

The problem that all of us face is that there is no other way to get to heaven but through our acceptance of what Jesus has done for us.

> Jesus said to him, "I am the way, and the truth, and the life; no one comes to the Father, but by me."
>
> John 14:6 (NIV)

The first step toward knowing our eternal state is realizing we cannot make it to heaven on our own. We all need a savior. You also need to commit your life and allegiance to this Savior, for He paid a very high price for your sins.

If you have never asked Jesus into your life, you can do so now. Before you read the rest of this book, you need to first make your peace with the very God who willingly sacrificed His life in payment for your sins. You need to connect with the God now, for your eternity depends on it.

The Prayer of Salvation:

"Jesus, I realize that I was born into this world a sinner and that in my life I have continually fallen short. I acknowledge that I can not do anything on my own to obtain Your favor, for I am truly lost in my own sin. I have followed the darkness many times in my life, and I now stand before You guilty as charged, deserving Your righteous judgment.

Heavenly Father, I acknowledge that You sent Your only begotten son, Jesus, to sacrifice His life for my sins. He paid the ultimate price for my wickedness. I am awestruck at the love that You have shown me by that very act of sacrifice and love. I believe that Jesus died for me according to Your Word and now ask Him to come into my heart as Lord and Savior of my life. Please transform me from this wicked state and fill me with the Holy Spirit. Guide my understanding of Your Word and show me Your purpose for my life so that I may follow Your teachings forever.

Thank you for loving me, Jesus. Amen."

Welcome, dear brother or sister in Christ. Welcome into God's grace and forgiveness. Now it is time to move forward. If you are a first-time believer or just a person of faith that wants to renew their life with Jesus, I will provide you some instruction on what to do next in Appendix A of this book. Keep in mind the following:

> For by grace you have been saved through faith; and this is not your own doing, it is the gift of God.
>
> Ephesians 2:8 (NIV)

By your prayer and confession of faith, you have just accepted the gift of God, nothing more, nothing less. Rejoice! You have just passed from death unto life through Christ Jesus, our Lord. You have crossed the darkness into light, and all of heaven rejoices!

Jesus Also Wants to Restore Our Nation

Many in this country are unaware that we are already heading down the path toward the Lord's judgment. Yet even as we are spiraling down this path due to our rebellion, our Savior is waiting to restore our nation and its people if we only repent (turn 180 degrees, have a change of mind and direction) our wickedness. Likewise, it should be the goal of our citizens and those of faith to restore this country and its people back to the track of "one nation under God."

> But, after they had rest (Israel was at peace during this time from many years of war), they did evil again before thee, and thou didst abandon them to the hand of their enemies, so that they had dominion over them; **yet when they turned and cried to thee thou didst hear from heaven, and many times thou didst deliver them according to thy mercies.**
>
> Nehemiah 9:28 (NIV)

This book serves as both a warning and an expression of hope to our country and the people who elect our officials and representatives that govern this nation. It is my prayer that you will take this reading seriously and that it will motivate you to reclaim what was taken away from the faithful. Keep in mind that even Jesus turned the tables on the money changers when the house of His Father was being desecrated (Matthew 21:13).

There is much that we can do within the laws governing our nation if the believers' churches of all denominations unite under a common cause. Our enemies and the enemies of our children are well-organized and united. However, take courage, for we outnumber them. Unfortunately, we have not figured that out yet.

Our Country Was Founded by Men of Faith

Contrary to popular belief, our country was not founded by deists, atheists, or agnostics, but by God-fearing men and women that set the standards by which our society should be governed. There are many within this country that would like for you to believe that there has always been a separation of church and state, which is contrary to the truth. This secular humanistic doctrine is widely proclaimed by ultra-left politicians, the news media, major organizations such as the ACLU, and others. The Supreme Court ruling on the separation of church and state was decided in 1947 without any precedent. Furthermore, if you look at the historical writings from our Founding Fathers, you will come to the following conclusion:

The Majority of Our Founding Fathers Were Christians!

The phrase "Founding Fathers" is a proper noun. It refers to a very specific group of people: the fifty-five delegates to the Constitutional Convention. Yes, there were other important players like Jefferson, whose thinking deeply influenced the

27

shape of our nation and who were not in attendance, but the fifty-five Fathers make up the core.[b]

The denominational affiliation of these men is a matter of public record. Among the delegates were twenty-eight Episcopalians, eight Presbyterians, seven Congregationalists, two Lutherans, two Dutch Reformed, two Methodists, two Roman Catholics, one unknown, and only three deists[c] — Williamson, Wilson, and Franklin — all this at a time when church membership entailed a sworn public confession of biblical faith.

This is a very revealing tally. It means that the members of the Constitutional Convention, the most influential group of men to shape the political foundations of our nation, were almost all Christians. Fifty-one out of fifty-five were Christians — a full ninety-three percent. Indeed, nearly twenty percent were Calvinists (the Presbyterians and the Dutch Reformed), considered by some to be the most extreme and dogmatic form of Christianity.[d]

Our Founding Fathers Were Driven to Protect and Embrace Christianity in Governance and in the Public Welfare of Our Country

George Washington, the father of our country, could not have stated it better in his memoirs:

> As the contempt of the religion of a country by ridiculing any of its ceremonies, or affronting its ministers or votaries, has ever been deeply resented, you are to be particularly careful to restrain every officer and soldier from such imprudence and folly, and to punish every instance of it. On the other hand, as far as lies in your power; you are to protect and support the free exercise of the religion of this country,

28

and the undisturbed enjoyment of the rights of conscience in religious matters, with your utmost influence and authority.

Every man conducting himself as a good citizen, and being accountable to God alone for his religious opinions, ought to be protected in worshipping the Deity according to the dictates of his own conscience... **If I could have entertained the slightest apprehension that the Constitution framed in the Convention, where I had the honor to preside, might possibly endanger the religious rights of any ecclesiastical Society, certainly I would never have placed my signature to it.**[e]

However, isn't that exactly what the Supreme Court did in 1947 when it ruled that the "walls for separation between church and state need to be high and impregnable?" The father of our country would not have signed the Constitution if he thought it would "endanger the religious rights" of our citizens. Yet each day, those of faith within our country are being stripped of their fundamental rights of religious expression. The "separation of church and state" ruling has set the precedent that the radical left has leveraged to suppress the churches of believers so that, if disagreement with governmental opinion is expressed within the churches, those in disagreement risk losing their not-for-profit status. The ACLU is on the forefront of these attacks with an internal policy goal of removing tax exempt statuses from the churches within this country[f]. Therefore, the churches are faced with taking a position of political correctness versus biblical truths within their teachings. What is noticeably absent within the church is any teaching regarding a heated position that is biblically accurate but may be contrary to a candidate or political position of authority. This is a direct violation of our freedom of speech, which the Constitution of the United States clearly protects. This is unacceptable.

It is no wonder that the majority of churches within this country are lukewarm rather than being on fire for God. It is also no wonder that the majority of believers who profess their faith in God sit idly by as the far left and secular humanist dominate our media, schools, and government with their anti-religious views, opinions, teachings, and laws. It is sad and ironic that those who take a stand for God's moral principals and societal norms (i.e. The Ten Commandments, The Golden Rule, etc.) are considered right-wing zealots! How far have we backslid as a country and nation that when a God-fearing and moral Supreme Court nominee such as John Roberts is ridiculed by liberal politicians and the media for being out of touch with the mainstream? The question remains, why isn't there a cry emanating from the masses of believers within this country saying that, **"We won't take it anymore"**?

The Constitution is very clear regarding the protection of religious freedoms and the expression thereof as revealed within the First Amendment, which states that:

> **Congress shall make no law** respecting an establishment of religion, **OR prohibiting the free exercise thereof**; **OR** abridging the freedom of speech, **OR** of the press; **OR** the right of the people peaceably to assemble, and to petition the Government for a redress of grievances.[g]

As a people, we are being prohibited from the "free exercise of religion" when our children are denied the right to proclaim "one nation under God" within our schools. Let's take that a step further. Not only are our children being denied their freedom of expression, they are also being forced to accept teachings within our educational system concerning alternative lifestyles under the guise of tolerance and evolution as fact versus theory. Where is the ACLU in its defense against the abuse of our civil liberties? Why must our children accept teachings that are contrary to our faith and belief system? Is that how this country assures "domestic tranquility"[h] by having the secular humanist brainwash our youth to accept obscure theories as fact and biblically-defined wickedness as a cultural norm?

Many secular humanists ignore the fact that over ninety-three percent of this nation's Founding Fathers were God-fearing men who intended to create a Christian nation by design. Instead, they often point to the three known deists, such as Benjamin Franklin, to support their warped views that somehow our nation was destined to exclude God from our society.

A *deist,* according to Dictionary.com, is one who holds "The belief, based solely on reason, in a God who created the universe and then abandoned it, assuming no control over life, exerting no influence on natural phenomena, and giving no supernatural revelation." Deists are usually anti-religion by nature and are often referred to as "chicken-hearted atheists."

Although Benjamin Franklin was known to be a deist, I find it fascinating that he supported religion as a governing force within our government and even proposed prayer during heated debate within the Constitutional Convention on June 28, 1787.

The debate on the floor over representation and voting had reached a hopeless deadlock, and tempers were heating up. Some of the New York delegation had already left, and others were on the verge of following suit. At this dismal and unpromising point of debate, the 81-year-old philosopher, scientist, and statesman rose to address President Washington and delegates.

As recorded by the convention's secretary, James Madison, here is what Franklin said:[i]

Mr. President,

The small progress we have made after four or five weeks' close attendance & continual reasoning's with each other – our different sentiments on almost every question, several of the last producing as many noes as ays, is methinks a melancholy proof of the imperfection of the human understanding. We have gone back to ancient history for models of government, and examined the different forms of those Republics which having been formed with the seeds of their own dissolution now no longer exist. And we have viewed modern states all round Europe, but find none of their Constitutions suitable to our circumstances.

In this situation of this Assembly, groping as it were in the dark to find political truth, and scarce able to distinguish it when presented to us, how has it happened, Sir, that we have not hitherto once thought of humbly applying to the Father of Lights to illuminate our understanding! In the beginning of the contest with Great Britain, when we were sensible of danger, we had daily prayer in this room for the Divine protection. Our prayers, Sir, were heard, and they were graciously answered. All of us who were engaged in the struggle must have observed frequent instances of a superintending Providence in our favor. To that kind providence, we owe this happy opportunity of consulting in peace on the means of establishing our future national felicity. **And have we now forgotten this powerful Friend? Or do we imagine we no longer need His assistance? I have lived, Sir, a long time, and the longer I live, the more convincing proofs I see of this truth—that God governs in the affairs of men.** And if a sparrow cannot fall to the ground without His notice, is it probable that an empire can rise without His notice, is it probable that an empire can rise without His aid? **We have been assured, Sir, in the Sacred Writings, that "except the Lord build the house, they labor in vain that build it". I firmly believe this; and I also believe that without His concurring aid, we shall succeed in this political building no better than the builders of Babel:** We shall be divided by our little partial local interest; our projects will be confounded; and we ourselves shall become a reproach and bye word down to future ages. And, what is worse, mankind may hereafter from this unfortunate instance, despair of establishing governments by human wisdom and leave it to chance, war, and conquest.

I therefore be leave to move—that henceforth prayers imploring the assistance of Heaven, and its blessings on our deliberations, be held in this Assembly every morning before we proceed to business, and that one or more of the clergy of this city be requested to officiate in that service. [j]

Consider the writing of Benjamin Franklin:

1. Due to the division within the Constitutional Convention, he acknowledged the result would be **"melancholy proof of the imperfection of the human understanding,"** without God's guidance.
2. Other nations from which the attendees were drawing examples (typically the secular enlightenment argument) were **formed with seed from their own dissolution.**
3. In all their efforts to come to consensus by their own reasoning, they neglected to seek guidance from the **"Father of Lights to illuminate their Understanding."** This is a poetic reference to God and the lack of forethought by these other nations to include God in their counsel.
4. Franklin brings up an example of when this country's people had their backs against the wall during the war with Britain. During this time, daily prayer for divine protection and guidance was a constant. Isn't that a sad truth on how we treat God today? How short-term our memory is regarding God's divine grace, mercy, and protection. Most often in the heat of battle, the reality of God is very real. Yet, shortly after the danger passes, we often respond to our Creator with faithless betrayal. Our nation did exactly that after World War II by throwing God out of our country via the separation of church and state ruling of 1947.
5. Franklin then reminds the assembled of Divine Providence to which those within the committee were witness: "All of us who were engaged in the struggle [with Britain] must have **observed frequent instances of a superintending Providence in our favor."**

6. He then makes his most famous statement of God's direct involvement, "And have we now forgotten this powerful Friend? Or do we imagine we no longer need His assistance? I have lived, Sir, a long time, and the longer I live, the more convincing proofs I see of this truth—that God governs in the affairs of men."

7. Using an analogy from Matthew 10:29: "Are not two sparrows sold for a penny? And not one of them will fall to the ground without your Father's will." Franklin then speaks to the rise and fall of any empire/nation that would succeed or fail based upon God's grace, knowledge, and will.

8. Franklin then uses the example of Genesis 11, the Tower of Babel, to illustrate what happens when man tries to rule under his own intellect. He also uses Psalm 127:1 to convince his colleagues that "Unless the LORD builds the house, those who build it labor in vain. Unless the LORD watches over the city, the watchman stays awake in vain."

9. **Franklin also served a warning that is very real today regarding a consequence of not being a "nation under God":**
   a We shall be divided by our little partial local interest
   b. Our projects will be confounded
   c. We shall become a reproach and byword in future ages
   d. Mankind may hereafter from this unfortunate instance despair of establishing governments by human wisdom and leave it to chance, war, and conquest.

10. In this concluding statement, Mr. Franklin rallied the cooperation of the convention participants and then galvanized their resolve by his recom-

mendation to open each day's assembly with "prayer," which was agreed upon and adopted as a standard practice to this very day.

It is ironic and a bit hypocritical that each day's session in Congress is opened with prayer, yet it is unconstitutional for a child to proclaim "one nation under God" in school. It is appalling that our senators, congressmen, and congresswomen sit back in silence while Chief Justice Roy Moore is suspended for refusing to remove the Ten Commandments from his court while a plaque of the Ten Commandments sits above the Supreme Court justices in their courtroom. It has become acceptable to dismiss a chief justice for not removing the Ten Commandments and tolerate judicial legislation by unelected jurists that totally disregards public outcry and protest. Throughout all of this, the Bible is clear about a nation that subscribes to this "God suppressive" mindset.

> Woe to those who call evil good and good evil, who put darkness for light and light for darkness.
>
> Isaiah 5:20 (NIV)

The United States of America is a backsliding nation in desperate need of repentance. Our Founding Fathers were men of faith who knew if we were ever to abandon God, we would inevitably fall into sin and iniquity. We would be a nation divided and unprotected by God. This is the current state of this country today. To make matters worse, our leaders are party-serving instead of people-serving. Our constitution is being ignored and misinterpreted without any real consequence or outpouring protest from the churches of believers. We have lost our zeal for God and have embraced sin as a cultural norm. We have thrown God out of every aspect of our government and are now indoctrinating our children with secular teachings found in our schools and colleges.

Woe to this nation indeed. We are a nation of people whose sin is increasing greatly with each year and generation. We will reap the consequences of our wickedness if we fail as a nation to:

1. Acknowledge our sinful state and hopelessness without God.
2. Realize that there is a consequence to our actions and that judgment will follow.
3. Remove those individuals from positions of authority who represent stumbling blocks to our religious freedoms.
4. Aggressively protest against those persons, business, agencies, and media organizations who are persecutors of our religious freedoms and their sponsors.
5. Reverse the 1947 ruling that imposed the "separation of church and state," and take this country back to a moral standard of being "one nation under God."
6. Get involved, physically, mentally, and spiritually.
7. Focus on honoring God more than man.

Acknowledging
Our Country's Sinful State

> Have nothing to do with the fruitless deeds of
> darkness, but **rather expose them.**
>
> Ephesians 5:11 (NIV)

When it comes to acts of wickedness and sin, we are commanded to "have nothing to do" with these "fruitless deeds." This does not mean we are to be isolationists, content within our own little world, safe from the outside.

Consider the aforementioned quote from Ephesians. You will notice that it does not give you a license to attack people perpetrating the deed, but instead you are *required* to expose the deeds or acts of darkness. This is a very important statement upon which the reader truly needs to reflect. People of faith are required to love their enemies (Matthew 5:44). However, true love takes action, and there are many forms of love. For example, we demonstrate love to our children by showing discipline when they are acting in a manner that is inappropriate and objectionable. As parents, we would not think twice about removing them from a position, circumstance, or action that may cause them or others harm. We are to act in the same way with regard to those whose actions are contrary to God's Word and whose objectives cause division and harm within this country.

God loves the sinner, but hates the sin. The very reason for Jesus' arrival on earth was to save those who were sick (Matthew 9:11-13). When you read on within this chapter, I will introduce you to the "fruitless deeds of darkness," which are destroying this country. Give care in considering the words "fruitless deeds" in this passage. A plant that does not bear fruit consumes the nutrients of the ground without producing food or sustenance to the farmer. The Bible provides an example of such a plant as being "tares," sown amongst the wheat. An interesting thing about a "tare" is that it looks like wheat, but it is a poisonous weed that bares no fruit with the exception of its own replication. If left to its own, it will eventually choke out the wheat.

> Another parable He put forth to them, saying: "The kingdom of heaven is like a man who sowed good seed in his field; but while men slept, his enemy [Satan] came and sowed tares among the wheat and went his way. [26] But when the grain had sprouted and produced a crop, then the tares also appeared. So the servants of the owner came and said to him, 'Sir, did you not sow good seed in your field? How then does it have tares?' He said to them, 'An enemy has done this.' The servants said to him, 'Do you want us then to go and gather them up?' But he said, 'No, lest while you gather up the tares you also uproot the wheat with them. Let both grow together until the harvest, and at the time of harvest I will say to the reapers, "First gather together

> the tares and bind them in bundles to burn
> them, but gather the wheat into my barn.'"
>
> Matthew 13:24-30 (NKJV)

Fruitless deeds such as sin and wickedness are consuming the moral fabric that has made this nation great.

The key in the following chapter is to realize and expose the sin and to make provision for the sinner to see the error of his/her ways in order to reach out to them for the kingdom of God. At the same time, we would never want to have a drunk get behind the wheel of a car out of fear that he could hurt or kill himself or someone else. Likewise, we need to stop those who are sowing the seeds of darkness within this country and within the legal and moral guidelines set forth in the Word of God. Knowing what to do requires an understanding of the problems within our country and how the Bible demands that we respond. As men and women of faith, we have a personal stake in the outcome. We cannot sit idly by and watch as God is ripped from the fabric of our country. We must put a stake in the ground to reverse this trend. It is critical to understand that we are one in a very large community of believers. If we unite under a common banner, we can make a difference.

The "fruitless deeds of darkness" are as follows.

The Fruitless Deeds of the ACLU

> Their throats are gaping graves, their tongues
> slick as mud slides. Every word they speak is
> tinged with poison.
>
> Romans 3:13 (The Message)

Harsh words for an organization that many Americans believe were created to protect our civil liberties. Contrary to popular belief, the ACLU was not a civil rights organization that somehow went bad over time. From the outset of its existence, its purpose was to undermine the very foundations of our democratic system while cloaked behind the American flag, civil liberties, and constitutional freedoms.

Background:

The ACLU was founded by Roger Baldwin, Crystal Eastman, Albert DeSilver, and others in 1920. The ACLU is a nonprofit and nonpartisan (so it claims) civil liberties organization that has grown from a roomful of civil liberties activists to an organization of more than five hundred thousand members and supporters. The ACLU handles nearly six thousand court cases annually from regional offices in almost every state.[k] The ACLU is a large organization with autonomous regional chapters embedded within each state reporting up to its corporate headquarters.

It is estimated that the ACLU has a net worth of 175 million dollars, with an annual budget of forty-five million dollars. It is heavily funded through a provision passed by Congress in 1976. The **"Civil Rights Attorneys Fee Award Act"** was established to encourage private lawyers to take on suits to protect civil and constitutional rights. The law provides that judges can order federal and state governments to pay legal fees to private lawyers who sue the government and win.

The ACLU has capitalized on this provision to bolster its revenue stream and operating budget. For example, if the ACLU wins a case that involves a public institution, the organization collects its full legal fees even if the attorneys offered their services without charge. Therefore, the **American taxpayer** funds a significant portion of the ACLU's operating budget through the thousands of court cases it litigates and wins each year! The remaining revenues generated by the ACLU are derived from their members and supporters.

The Founders of the ACLU:

The ACLU's founder, Roger Baldwin, was a professed communist who stated: "My chief aversion is the system of greed, private profit, privilege and violence which makes up control of the world today, and which has brought it to the tragic crisis of unprecedented hunger and unemployment... **Therefore, I am for Socialism, disarmament and ultimately, for the abolishing of the State itself**... I seek the social ownership of property, the abolition of the propertied class and sole control of those who produce wealth."

Baldwin's early friend was the radical anarchist, Emma Goldman, whom he considered a mentor. Goldman has been described as a consistent promoter of anarchism, radical education, free love, and birth control. Her advocacy of these causes led to her nickname "Red Emma." She conspired to kill Henry Clay Frick of Carnegie Steel, founded the anarchist magazine *Mother Earth*, and was eventually deported to Russia in 1919. According to the online exhibit of Goldman's papers, her ideas led to the "founding of the American Civil Liberties Union," and her career served as an inspiration for Baldwin.[l]

What Baldwin also learned from Goldman was how to mask his true agenda and disguise it in a way to get the elites on his side. This would be a strategy that Baldwin and the ACLU would repeatedly use to gain access to funding from the wealthy, while at the same time working to destroy many of the core values of the free enterprise system that led to the creation of their wealth.[m]

This is the foundation and founding principle of the ACLU that has been carried over throughout the years and is supported widely by the secular humanist sect within the United States. The actions of the ACLU have been extremely detrimental to our country's culture, our belief system, the laws protecting our people, and to all religions — especially the Judeo-Christian tradition that is historically rooted within our nation.

Many believe that the ACLU had a righteous beginning and was the primary advocate for protecting the civil liberties within this country. While researching the "fruitless deeds" of the ACLU, I was truly surprised to find a secular humanistic and socialist history stemming back eighty years to its inception. Cloaked within the pretense of civil liberties, the ACLU has successfully followed the path of least resistance by leveraging liberal judges to rule and judicially create law to circumvent the will of the people, establish new precedents in constitutional law, and undermine our constitution through their warped, liberal, and somewhat elitist interpretations and views.

If I were to focus on all of the "fruitless deeds" of the ACLU, I would be able to write an entire book on this topic alone. That said, I highly encourage you to read *The ACLU vs. America – Exposing the Agenda to Redefine Moral Values* by Alan Sears and Craig Osten for a more in-depth presentation of the ACLU's agenda. For the purposes of this book, I will focus on a number of recent and historical events that demonstrate the ACLU's agenda and how it has and continues to undermine the moral fabric of this country — in most cases in stark contrast to the will of the people.

If you look at the root cause of the moral downfall within this country, you will notice that the ACLU used a tactic to chip away at the foundations of faith that allowed us to grow and be blessed as a nation.

> When the foundations are being destroyed, what can the righteous do?
>
> Psalm 11:3 (NIV)

This country's strength has and will always be in a foundation of God-centered morality, which was the basis for the development of our constitution. We were once a "nation under God," whereby our moral foundation was very solid and well established. It is this foundation that provides shape to all of the pillars of strength in governance and in which the "blessings of liberty and domestic tranquility" are rooted.

Today, it is this foundation that has been attacked and redefined by the litigious successes of the ACLU in support of the liberal media, the entertainment industry, and left-wing politicians. So the question arises: What are the moral underpinnings that are foundational necessities within the United States of America? To answer that question properly, one must consider that which is important to God.

How do we view our existence in relation to God? How do we value and respect life? How do we protect the poor and innocent? How do we define love and relationships? And, most importantly, how do we connect with God? These are the foundational pinions that have made the United States of America a great nation.

In contrast, you will notice that the removal or mitigation of each foundational underpinning results in a negative moral consequence. This consequence is the catalyst for the ACLU to establish a footing for the next level of attack in a purposeful and planned strategy to deteriorate this country's moral values. This consequence has and will continue to foster a national policy of separation of our children and our families from their Creator. Consider the following and give special attention to the linkages that the ACLU has constructed to the detriment of America by embracing and promulgating these beliefs, norms, laws, and internal policies:

1) **Evolution vs. Creationism** - If the existence of the earth and man can be explained by evolution and natural selection, then a secular humanistic world opens up where we, as a people and society, are subject only to the authority governing us at the

45

time. Therefore, good and evil are only relative to the individual's interpretation and belief system. This is the basis for the viewpoint that "what is good for you may be justifiably evil to someone that does not share your view." God is taken out of the equation, for we are not held accountable to a supreme being. If you believe in evolution, mankind is reduced to a complex animal that is influenced by a bunch of genes, hormones, and societal conditions.

2) **Sanctity of Life** - Abortion is a very big topic within this country, with "freedom of choice" being the constitutional right set forth in the United States Supreme Court's 1973 decision in *Roe vs. Wade.* This choice has collectively resulted in over forty-two million abortions to date—the equivalent of the population of California or the country of Canada.[n] If you have a secular humanistic viewpoint, abortion is a fundamental right with no consequence. However, God's view is starkly different:

> For you created my inmost being; you knit
> me together in my mother's womb.
> Psalm 139:13 (NIV)

In God's view, conception is the beginning of life and being known intimately by God Himself.

Euthanasia is another issue concerning the sanctity of life. The evolutionary mindset leads to the view that we are just animals that have evolved and thus have no consequence. Life is not sacred anymore, and natural selection, survival of the fittest, and other rational justifications dictate that abortion and euthanasia are logical solutions to poverty, hopelessness, and individual mistakes and bad choices.

3) **Protecting the Poor and Innocent** – When the ACLU endorses policies that legalize prostitution, protects the distribution of child pornography, supports a position that parents have no legal recourse to shield their children from pornography, defends (free of charge) the North American Man-Boy Love Association (NAMBLA) against a civil suit arising out of the hideous rape and murder of a ten-year-old boy,[o] it all begs the question: How in the world are the actions of the ACLU, purported to be on behalf of this country's civil liberties, in any way "establishing justice, ensuring domestic tranquilly and promoting the general welfare" as stated within the Preamble to the Constitution of the United States of America?[p]

4) **The Redefinition of Marriage** – Peter Singer, chair of Princeton University's Center for Human Values, wrote an article titled "Heavy Petting," which defends bestiality, or sexual relations between humans and animals. He wrote: "We are all animals, indeed more specifically, we are great apes. This does not make sex across the species barrier normal, or natural, whatever those much-misused words may mean, but it does imply that it ceases to be an offense to our status and dignity as human beings."[q] Consider what Singer is saying. If you were to embrace the belief that we evolved from slime to man, then man is just an animal, and, thus, all forms of love and sex, albeit heterosexual, same sex, polygamy, bestiality, and pedophilia, are acceptable, for there is no distinction from one form of love to another. The definition of marriage now becomes blurred, because God is no longer the authority or standard for its defi-

nition, which comes instead from the federal and state governments and the courts.

5) Religious Persecution and Oppression – Never in my wildest dreams would I have thought that the United States of America would persecute its citizens' rights of religious expression under the guise of constitutional protection. The terms "separation of church and state" and the "Separation Clause" are loosely used by the ACLU to defend their anti-American agenda. It is ironic that while the ACLU promotes tolerance to alternate lifestyle teachings and has even litigated that such teachings be mandatory within the Kentucky school system, it brands stating "Merry Christmas" on a state college campus unconstitutional.

As previously mentioned, the "separation of church and state" Supreme Court Ruling of 1947 was the result of the ACLU's successful ploy to move this country away from the common law at that time, which was God-centric, to that of a secular humanistic policy and mindset. This was a huge victory for the ACLU and the catalyst to the suppression of religious freedoms. Today, the ACLU is attacking the US Military to prevent the Boy Scouts from assembling on military bases. These are the children of families stationed on military installations. In addition, military chaplains are now being suppressed from mentioning Jesus while in military uniform. As I am writing this book, Navy Chaplain Klingenschmitt is presently on a hunger strike in front of the White House after being ordered by navy admirals not to pray publicly in Jesus' name unless he is wearing civilian clothes.

The bottom line is that when it comes to civil liberties and constitutional freedoms, the ACLU makes Bin Laden look like Mother Teresa. When you consider what the ACLU has done to this country from a cultural norm and morality standpoint, one wonders why the people of this country are allowing this to happen. These fruitless deeds have resulted in legal rulings and actions that are in opposition to the moral standards by which this country was founded. As a result, their misguided contributions are heading this country down the path of God's judgment.

To recap, the following is just a short list of the cases and policies of the ACLU that had the most detrimental impact upon our country:

1. The legalization of prostitution (Policy 211).
2. All legal prohibitions on the distribution of obscene material, including child pornography, are unconstitutional (Policy 4d, 4g).
3. Pornography outlets can be wherever they please, whether next to churches, daycare centers, or near residential neighborhoods (Policy 4e).
4. Tax-funded libraries cannot restrict the access of children to all forms of pornography on the Internet.[r]
5. Parents should have **no legal recourse** in shielding their children from exposure to hard-core pornography (Policy 2a).
6. The military cannot enforce even the most basic codes of conduct, such as discipline for disrespectful behavior towards a superior officer (Policy 39a).
7. The military cannot stop open displays of homosexual behavior within its ranks, even though there is a standing policy against any public display of affection irrespective of sexual preference.[s]
8. The decriminalization and legalization of all drugs (Policy 210).

9. The promotion of homosexuality to include the mandatory training of our children within the public school venue under the guise of tolerance (Policy264).
10. Parents cannot limit their children's exposure to or participation in the public school classes and assemblies regarding any topic—except Orthodox Jewish or Christian teachings, even when the teachings violate the family's core religious and moral beliefs (Policy 62a).'
11. Opposition to rating of music and movies (Policy 18).
12. Opposition to requiring parental consent to a minor obtaining an abortion.
13. Opposition to requiring spousal consent preceding abortion (Policy 262).
14. Opposition to requiring informed consent preceding abortion (Policy 263).
15. Opposition to parental choice in children's education (Policy 80).
16. Abolition of all legislative, military, and prison chaplaincy programs (Policy 88, 89).
17. Repeal of all criminal and civil laws that prohibit polygamy and same-sex "marriage" (Policy 91).
18. Opposition to the right of any lawful possession of firearms by citizens, except by law enforcement officials (Policy 47).

And the list goes on…

The Fruitless Deeds of Evolution

Since the creation of the world, God's invisible qualities—his eternal power and divine nature—have been clearly seen, being understood from what has been made, **so that men are without excuse.** For, although they knew God, they neither glorified him as God nor gave thanks to him, but their thinking became futile and their foolish hearts were darkened.

Romans 1:20-21

A Nation Brainwashed by Evolutionary Theory

If you are like most Americans, you have been brought up learning about the origins of man, Darwinism, and evolution from grade school to college. The lead scientists of the world have painted a compelling picture of how the universe was created, how the earth formed billions of years ago, and how life evolved from the amoeba to that of the modern man.

When you consider the fossil records, you are led to believe that it must have taken billions of years for the earth to evolve into the world we live in today. Today, most scientists would agree that the earth has to be approximately four and a half billion years old for evolution to have played out properly. Yet, the following pages will illustrate that what you have been taught in the past simply does not hold up to true scientific scrutiny.

You may be asking, what's the big scandal? These scientists are the professionals, skilled in critical analysis, without bias, and with a focus on the facts. Why would leading scientists agree to evolutionary theory if it were not true? Consider the following:

I will not accept that philosophically (creation), because I do not want to believe in God, therefore I choose to believe in that

which I know is scientifically impossible,
spontaneous generation arising to evolution.

> Dr. George Wald, evolutionist,
> Professor Emeritus of Biology
> at the University at Harvard,
> Nobel Prize winner in Biology.

My attempts to demonstrate evolution by
an experiment carried on for more than 40
years have completely failed.....It is not even
possible to make a caricature of an evolution
out of paleobiological facts...The idea of an
evolution rests on pure belief.

> Dr. Nils Heribert-Nilsson,
> noted Swedish botanist and
> geneticist at Lund University

Think about it for a moment. If there is an intelligent
Creator that put all of this together, is it possible that we may
be accountable to that Creator? People do not like the idea
that they are not in control, especially the elitists among us.
Explaining away the truth by speculative theories that just
don't measure up to the empirical evidence is more believ-
able than admitting that God put this together. Therefore,
scientists are left to believe in a lie that results in no consequence. If you subscribe to this belief, then mankind is free
from divine accountability. The alternative is to believe in a
truth that puts God back into the forefront of our lives.

The greatest fear of the ACLU, the secular humanists,
the evolutionist, and the liberal left is that the people of this
country may embrace the idea that God created this world
and mankind and that evolution is the greatest hoax of the
century. The following pages will demonstrate that the

scientific theories you have grown up believing are heavily flawed.

Let's begin with the basics—the foundation of evolutionary theory, which claims that simple cells evolved from a pool of slime to man over a very long period of time.

There's No Such Thing as a Simple Cell...

Molecular biology has shown that even the simplest of all living systems on earth today, bacterial cells, are exceedingly complex objects. Although the tiniest bacterial cells are incredibly small, weighing less than 10^{-12}gms, each is in effect a veritable microminiaturized factory containing thousands of exquisitely designed pieces of intricate molecular machinery, made up altogether of **one hundred thousand million atoms,** far more complicated than any machine built by man and absolutely without parallel in the nonliving world.

Molecular biology has also shown that the basic design of the cell system is essentially the same in all living systems on earth from bacteria to mammals. In all organisms, the roles of DNA, MRNA, and protein are identical. The meaning of the genetic code is also virtually identical in all cells. **The size, structure and component design of the protein synthetic machinery is practically the same in all cells. In terms of their basic biochemical design, therefore, no living system can be thought of as being primitive or ancestral with respect to any other**

system, nor is there the slightest empirical hint of an evolutionary sequence among all the incredibly diverse cells on earth. For those who hoped that molecular biology might bridge the gulf between chemistry and biochemistry, the revelation was profoundly disappointing.[u]

In the words of Monod:[v]

…we have no idea what the structure of a primitive cell might have been. The simplest living system known to us, the bacterial cell…in its overall chemical plan is the same as that of all other living beings. It employs the same genetic code and the same mechanism of translation as do, for example, human cells. Thus the simplest cells available to us for study **have nothing "primitive" about them**… no vestiges of truly primitive structures are discernable.

Too Complex for Random Chance to Create a Simple Cell

To further illustrate the complexity of a cell, consider their construction. One of the basic building blocks of a cell includes protein molecules, which are very complex in design. Furthermore, there could be thousands of protein molecules depending upon the cell. To add to this complexity, picture one protein cell. Amino acids comprise one of the subcomponents of a protein cell and are organized in a manner to create a complex protein molecule. As a result, in order for a basic living cell to exist, all of the right combinations of amino acids must be present to create one complex protein molecule. Then all of the protein molecules must align exactly in the correct sequence for the cell to work. If just one protein molecule were missing or misaligned, the cell would cease to function. The probabilities that this complex construction could come about by random chance are so astronomical that it is actually comical to consider it seriously. It would be equivalent to having an explosion within a Chevy plant, and the end result is the creation of a Corvette.

To illustrate the improbability that life sprung into existence out of raw materials in order to create one very basic cell, which, of course, begs the question of the origin of these raw materials, consider the following examples that put this into perspective from a mathematical standpoint.

According to leading scientists, the earth is four and a half billion years old, which is the general consensus. If you were to translate that into seconds, it would equate to the earth being approximately 14.2×10^{17} seconds old (1,400,0 00,000,000,000,000 seconds). Given that the probability of the correct arrangements of amino acids randomly organizing themselves into one complex protein molecule and of that molecule finding other protein molecules to align perfectly into the simplistic bacterial cell is 1 in 10^{300} (10 with 300 zeros). The total number of seconds in the age of the earth is less by a factor of eighteen, or approximately eighty-one billion years, than the time needed for random chance to play out the creation of one living cell!

Let me illustrate the point further. The age of the universe is approximately 13.7 billion years, as measured since the Big Bang got everything going, which represents approximately 10^{48} seconds.[w] In this same example, there have not been enough seconds since the beginning of the universe to illustrate the time necessary for random chance to create the most simplistic bacterial cell.

Furthermore, Dr. Emile Borel first formulated the basic Law of Probability, which states that, when the likelihood that an event will occur is beyond 1 chance in 10^{50} (the 200th power is used for scientific calculations), it can be said with certainty that the event will never happen, regardless of the time allotted or how many opportunities could exist for the event to take place.[x]

Keep in mind that the aforementioned calculations illustrate the probability that only one living cell could form spontaneously. It seems to me that it takes an incredible amount of faith for the evolutionists to believe in what they are preaching, for there is no empirical evidence to support it.

> It is my conviction that if any professional biologist will take adequate time to examine carefully the assumptions upon which the macro-evolution doctrine rests, and the observational and laboratory evidence that bears on the problem of origins, he/she will conclude that there are substantial reasons for doubting the truth of this doctrine. Moreover, I believe that a scientifically sound creationist view of origins is not only possible, but it is to be preferred over the evolutionary one.
>
> Dean H. Kenyon,
> Professor of Biology at
> San Francisco State University

Now, you may be wondering that if life did not evolve from the amoeba to man, what about the fossil records that provide a basis for the "origins of man," dinosaurs, and other extinct creatures? By observation, it would seem that the earth is billions of years old and that evolution has its place in our history. However, by examining the scientific evidence more closely, we find that this assumption is also without basis.

Fossil Records Don't Lie

I agree that fossil records don't lie. However, I also believe that many scientists have not been the most truthful and forthcoming in their research.

> "Darwin's evolutionary explanation of the origins of man has been transformed into a modern myth, to the detriment of scientific and social progress... The secular myths of evolution have had a damaging effect on scientific research, leading to distortion, to needless controversy, and to gross misuse of science... I mean the stories, the narratives about change over time. How the dinosaurs became extinct, how the mammals evolved, where man came from. These seem to me to be little more than story-telling."
>
> "If I knew of any Evolutionary transitional's, fossil or living, I would certainly have included them in my book, 'Evolution.'"
>
> Dr. Colin Patterson, Evolutionist and Senior Paleontologist at the British Museum of Natural History, which houses 60 million fossils

There is plenty of evidence within the fossil records that indicate the earth we live in is actually rather young and an intelligent designer (God) put this all together. If evolution were true, the fossil records would show transitional creatures of all sorts evolving into more complex creatures and new species over a very long period of time. However, if creationism is true, one would expect that the fossil records would reveal an explosion of all sorts of life forms with no transitional creatures. What we find in the fossil records is that very explosion of life, especially during the Cambrian period.

Most major animal groups appeared for the first time in the fossil records some 545 million years ago in a relatively short period of time known as the Cambrian explosion. The explanation of this sudden, apparent explosion persists today as a shadowy mystery. During the Cambrian explosion, which lasted a relatively short period of five million to ten million years, a huge number of complex, multi-celled organisms appeared. Moreover, this burst of animal forms led to most of the major animal groups we know today.[y] The Cambrian period is very disturbing to the evolutionist on two major fronts. First, the varieties of complex creatures just appeared out of nowhere within this strata with no evidence of any transitional creatures mutating into other more complex species.

> The facts of paleontology seem to support creation and the flood rather than evolution. For instance, all the major groups of invertebrates appear "suddenly" in the first fossil ferrous strata (Cambrian) of the earth with their distinct specializations indicating that they were all created almost at the same time.
>
> Professor Hannington Enoch,
> University of Madras

Modern Dating Methods Just Don't Add Up

So much has been said about the accuracy of the modern dating methods, such as Radio Carbon 14 and Potassium-Argon (K-Ar) Radiometric Dating, that one is led to believe that the Earth is truly very old. However, you seldom hear about the inaccuracies of these dating systems, especially when catastrophic conditions occur which will negatively influence their results, such as the global flood mentioned in the Bible.

While studying the various methods by which scientists date rocks, sediment layers, and fossils, I was amazed by the degree to which assumptive reasoning is relied upon in using these methods. I found that not all specimens are dated via the systems mentioned above. In many cases, when rocks are dated, assumptions are made based upon the surrounding fossil or the strata level by which they have been found.[z] For example, a sediment layer is presumed to be approximately one hundred million years old if fossils are embedded within it have been previously predated or the other way around. A fossil is then judged to be one hundred million years old because the sediment layer is so many feet deep and, thus, it must be so many years old. While these may be logical assumptions, they do not hold up to scientific scrutiny when considered in light of recent recorded events.

Consider the following:

> Recent observations and experiments demon-strate that sedimentation and sedimentary rock can also form very rapidly. Much in this regard was learned from the Mount St. Helens eruption on May 18, 1980. Located in Washington, this volcano deposited 25 feet of finely layered sediment around its base in just six hours.

> Furthermore, experiments by several different scientists show that differently sized particles within sediment can quickly sort themselves into layers like those found in sedimentary rock today. To these layers, add time and

pressure from the earth above and the result is sedimentary rock.[aa]

The Mount St. Helens volcano exploded with the force of 20,000 Hiroshima-sized atom bombs. One aftermath of the eruption was a 140-foot-deep canyon that was formed in just one day. At that rate, the entire Grand Canyon could have been formed in only forty days; not 40 million years! Observation since the eruption has revealed new rock layered strata similar to the walls of the Grand Canyon, forming at the rate of 100 feet per year. In one case, such a wall descended 25 feet in depth over just one day.[bb]

Another example of how we should be rethinking sedimentary and other strata ageing methods is evident from the following:

Lin Ottinger, Moab back-country tour guide and amateur geologist and archaeologist, made a find early last week that could upset all current theories concerning the age of mankind on this planet. While searching for mineral specimens south of Moab, Ottinger found traces of human remains in a geological stratum that is approximately 100 million years old.... He carefully uncovered enough of what later proved to be parts of two human skeletons.

Of course, despite evidence that these human remains are 'in place' in a formation 100 million years old, the probability is very low that they are actually that old. The bones appeared to be relatively modern in configuration that is of Homo sapiens rather than one of his ancient, semi-animal predecessors.[cc]

To recap, sediment layers can be duplicated by recent catastrophic events, which would support a young earth theory. This is problematic, considering how fossils and rocks are dated by scientists. Additionally, skeleton remains, which are intermixed within a stratum that is dated one hundred million years old, create a significant problem within the scientific community. For such findings predate the "origins of man" timeline by approximately ninety-five million years! The evidence suggests that the current methods of geological dating are heavily flawed, thus deserving critical assessment and reevaluation.

To add more complexity to this subject, the actual dating methods have their own failures, which include:

Carbon 14 Shortcomings:

Dr. Willard F. Libby invented the carbon 14 dating method, which he developed during the late '40s and early '50s. He won a Nobel Prize for his excellent work. He wrote in his book, however, that carbon 14 dating is only accurate to about four thousand years. After that amount of time, the system becomes unreliable.[dd] It also seems that when water is introduced to the equation, this method of dating becomes highly inaccurate. For example, the Radiocarbon analysis of a <u>freshly killed seal</u> at McMurdo had an apparent age of thirteen hundred years.[ee] Also according to Radiocarbon dating, living snails from the Southern Nevada Springs "died" twenty-seven thousand years ago.[ff]

Potassium-Argon (K-Ar) Radiometric Method Shortcomings:

In the case of Mount Saint Helens, the volcano was obviously formed in 1986 when it cooled. But examination with the potassium-argon (K-Ar) radiometric method determined it to be as many as three hundred and fifty thousand years old, give or take fifty thousand years. [gg]

These are only a few examples of the shortcomings regarding the "so-called," "extremely accurate" dating methods used today. When the "origins of man" is considered, it gets much, much worse.

Man Did Not Evolve from an Ape...

> Often, a cold shudder has run through me, and I have asked myself whether I may have not devoted myself to a fantasy.
>
> Charles Darwin,
> Life and Letters,
> 1887, Vol. 2, p. 229

There are significant flaws within the "origins of man" fossil records, including the methods used in scientific discovery that have cast serious doubt on its authenticity. As you will notice from the following examples, there is a sect within the scientific community that is biased towards accepting evolution as fact. Many scientists who have devoted their lives towards critical assessment have ignored the evidence against evolution. Some have even doctored specimens to serve their cause.

To understand better how evolution evolved in our culture, we must go back to the early '20s. The ACLU's legal support and determination to have evolutionary theory taught within our schools were the catalysts for the acceptance of this theory within our country.

On May 3, 1925, the ACLU discussed the Tennessee anti-evolution act during a board meeting in New York. The board decided to issue a press announcement that it was willing to support any teacher who supported evolution and would challenge the law's constitutionality. As a result of the ACLU's support for evolution, John Scopes came to the ACLU table to pursue a case for evolution within our courts. The famous case of the Scopes Monkey Trial was the beginning of an 81-year old hoax that we have been brainwashed to believe.

Scope's Monkey Trial of 1925 - The ACLU advertised and provided support to John T. Scopes (1900–70), a high school teacher who was charged with teaching Charles Darwin's theory of evolution, which violated a state law prohibiting the teaching of any doctrine that denied the divine creation of humans. The trial was broadcast live on radio and attracted worldwide interest. The prosecutor was William Jennings Bryan. The defense attorney was Clarence Darrow. The judge limited arguments to the basic charge to avoid a test of the law's constitutionality and a discussion of Darwin's theory. Scopes was found guilty and fined one hundred dollars, although he was later acquitted during a retrial on the technicality that he had been fined excessively. The law was repealed in 1967.[hh]

The "Tooth Fossil," which was also known as the "Nebraska Man," was believed by Mr. Scopes to be evolutionary proof of man's origin being traced back to the ape. Artists created renditions of the Nebraska Man to include communities of this missing link, as the world looked on in amazement and creation was put on the shelf based on the finding of a **single tooth fossil**. Ironically, this very tooth that John Scopes held up in court, which he proclaimed to be proof of man's evolution, was found in 1927 to be that of an extinct pig. Nevertheless, the support for evolutionary theory became a major pillar of division within our country and eventually resulted in the current prohibition of other theories, such as creation or intelligent design. This was the first major and highly publicized victory credited to the ACLU.

The ACLU is content to have our schools teach the theory of evolution, but not creationism or intelligent design. They are trying to remove any reference to the possibility that God may have had something to do with the creation of life as we know it. As you shall see later in this chapter, the ACLU and the education system do not even dispute the hoaxes associated with the "origins of man" that are still being taught in our schools and universities today. As a result, our society can be fed the lies that assert that man evolved from slime (the amoeba-to-man theory), which in turn gives credence to the claim that good and evil are in relative terms due to our animalistic history.

The "Scientific Method," which is the basis of scientific discovery, has been abandoned to support a highly biased and theoretical viewpoint. Furthermore, any contrary theory that may suggest a supreme designer, even though backed by scientific discovery, is immediately dismissed, not because of the scientific evidence, but conveniently because of the "separation of church and state" doctrine. Any school that attempts to introduce the concept of "intelligent design" is immediately pounced upon by the ACLU and secular humanist community under the expedient shroud of the Separation Clause. Those within the scientific community that embrace intelligent design due to the empirical evidence are either ostracized or portrayed as fanatics teaching religion.

The scientific community's position is neither science nor the protection of civil liberties, but rather censorship and forced teachings of an unfounded theory.

The Missing Link Is Still Missing...[ii]

As a child, I remember seeing a poster on the wall that demonstrated that man evolved from an ape by evolutionary transitions. To the far left of the poster was what looked like a pygmy chimpanzee, and on the far right was a modern man. Between them were the missing links with famous names, such as "Java Man," "Peking Man," "Neanderthal Man," and other such transitional creatures. For years, we have been brainwashed into believing that these were the true "origins of man." No one ever told us how each of these so-called transitional species of man has been debunked and that, in some cases, they were actual hoaxes, doctored by man and embraced by the scientific community.

The Nebraska Man: The *"Nebraska Man"* was fabricated from one unusual-looking tooth discovered in 1922. This tooth was supposed to signify what is depicted in an artist's drawing published in the *Illustrated London News* of 1922 (reproduced by Brown on page 11). Nebraska Man and his wife look distinctly ape-like in the drawing, but nevertheless, they faded away after 1927, when it was demonstrated that the tooth belonged to an extinct pig.

Ramapithecus: *"Ramapithecus,"* has been known for certain since 1978 to have been "just an ape with no linkage to man." Brown (p. 50) quotes Roger Lewin in *Bones of Contention* as remarking: "The dethroning of Ramapithecus - from putative first human in 1961 to extinct relative of the orangutan in 1982 - is one of the most fascinating, and bitter, sagas in the search for human origins."

Australopithecines: The *"Australopithecines,"* which arose in the minds of anthropologists from bones found in South Africa by Dr. Raymond Dart in 1924, were imagined as being "large-jawed, small-brained, standing about four feet tall and walking in approximately human fashion, not yet men but a pre-human phase of hominid evolution."[iii] Brown

(p. 11) cites recent studies which indicate that they are instead an extinct species of apes that did not walk upright or show any other human characteristics.

Java Man: *"Pithecanthropus erectus"* ("Java man") was introduced to an international congress of zoologists by Eugene Dubois in 1895. It arose in the researcher's imagination from a skullcap and a human thighbone found thirty-nine feet apart. **Dubois did not tell the congress that he had found in the same stratum two decidedly human skulls as well as parts of four other thighbones of apes.** After forty-two years of notoriety, he finally admitted in 1937 that "Java man" was just a large gibbon: "Pithecanthropus was not a man, but a gigantic genus allied to the Gibbons." (Brown, p. 51)

Piltdown Man: The *"Piltdown man"* is now "universally acknowledged to have been a hoax, and yet it was in textbooks for more than forty years" (Brown, p. 11). At Piltdown in England, Charles Dawson found during four years of excavations from 1908 to 1912 a human skullcap and, nearby, a broken lower jawbone which was ape-like, except that its teeth showed human wearing down. An important canine tooth was missing. In 1913, Teilhard de Chardin found the canine tooth. In 1915, Dawson claimed a similar find two miles distant. **This ape-man, estimated to have lived five hundred thousand years ago, was unmasked after forty years, when it was proven by tests that the jawbone belonged to an ape that had died recent to the reported finding and that the teeth had been filed down by modern hands as well as stained with chemicals to make them look more ancient.**[kk]

Peking Man: *"Sinanthropus"* (*"Peking man"*) was "discovered" by Dr. Davidson Black, Dr. Pei, and others in 1927. From a molar tooth and a skull, Dr. Black made a model according to his own imagination and the hopes of the Rockefeller Foundation, which was providing a yearly grant of twenty thousand dollars for the research. Father Patrick

O'Connell, who was in China at the time and studied the results as minutely as possible, concluded that Dr. Black had set out to produce a new species of ape-man from the evidence of a single tooth, confident that "the public he had in view would not be too exacting in demanding proofs."[11] Teilhard de Chardin was with Dr. Black as an observer and helped to build up the image. The suspicious circumstances of the site, located on a human lime-quarry and kiln, and the presence of **human bones were not properly reported. The reality is that they found modern human bones coexisting with the Peking Man. Furthermore, the back of the skulls of the Peking Man were bashed in with the contents drained out.** All the evidence for this new species of ape-man mysteriously disappeared in the '40s. According to O'Connell, the fraud of "Peking man" was discovered in France in the '40s, when all of the data regarding the case were carefully compared. **Brown summarizes the matter by noting that many experts today consider these bones to have been the remains of monkeys, which were consumed as food by men working long ago at the lime quarry.**

Neanderthal Man: For a century, the "Neanderthal Man" was depicted by artists as stooped and ape-like, based partly upon the remains of some individuals who had been afflicted with bone diseases, probably arthritis. Recent studies show that "Neanderthal man, Heidelberg man, and Cro-Magnon man were completely human" and stood just as erect as modern men do (Brown, p. 11).

Brown (p. 51) summarizes the scientific value of these alleged discoveries with a quote from W.R. Thompson in his introduction to *The Origin of Species*: "The success of Darwinism was accompanied by a decline in scientific integrity... A striking example, which has only recently come to light, is the alteration of the Piltdown skull so that it could be used as evidence for the descent of man from the apes; but even before then a similar instance of tinkering with evidence was finally revealed by the discoverer of Pithecanthropus [Java man], who admitted, many years after his sensational report, that he had found in the same deposits bones that are definitely human."

As my dear friend David Moore from "Moore on Life" has expressed time and again about the "origins of man," which is worth repeating now, **"If you believe that man evolved, then somebody's making a monkey out of you!"** This is precisely the garbage that we have been spoon-fed for years without any public outcry to the contrary.

The Fruitless Deeds of Abortion

The subject of abortion is very heated and crosses both religious and secular boundaries. There is a good chance that you, the reader, may have had an abortion or know a loved one or friend who has gone through this procedure. If that person is you, it is very important that you know that God loves you. We are all sinners, and the wages of sin is death, for all have sinned and have fallen short of the glory of God. There is no exception. That is precisely why Jesus came to this earth, so that we could have life through his sacrifice on the cross for our personal failings. Jesus was the sacrificial lamb for all of humanity's sins. He paid the price for all of our shortcomings the day he was nailed to that cross.

Therefore, I do not accuse or chastise those who have had an abortion. Nor am I writing this as ammunition for the ultra-right, who are determined to attack the person that has had an abortion. I am writing this to elevate the level of awareness and state the facts of how this "freedom of choice" mindset has masked a terrible reality.

Call it freedom of choice. Call it a woman's right to choose. The reality is that, within the United States of America, over forty-seven million abortions have been performed since the *Roe v. Wade* Supreme Court decision in

1973. **Worldwide, over forty-two million abortions are performed each year**, which translates to approximately one hundred and twenty-six thousand abortions per day.^{mm} This is a national and worldwide tragedy without equal.

Who's having abortions (age)?

Studies have shown 52% that women obtaining abortions in the United States are younger than twenty-five years old. Women aged 20-24 obtain 32% of all abortions. Teenagers obtain 20% and girls under 15 account for 1.2%.

Who's having abortions (religion)?

Women who are Protestant obtain 37.4 % of all abortions in the United States. Catholic women account for 31.3%, Jewish women account for 1.3%, and women with no religious affiliation obtain 23.7% of all abortions. Furthermore, 18% of all abortions are performed on women who identify themselves as "Born-again/Evangelical."

Therefore, those professing a belief in God account for approximately 76% of all abortions within the United States of America.

Why do women have abortions?

It is estimated that 1% of all abortions occur because the pregnancy was the result of rape or incest. Six percent (6%) of abortions occur because of potential health problems regarding either the mother or child. Therefore, over **93% of all abortions occur for social reasons** (i.e. the child is unwanted or inconvenient).

How likely it is that someone will have an abortion within the United States?

An estimated 43% of all women will have at least one abortion by the time they are 45 years old. Forty-seven percent (47%) of all abortions are performed on women who have had at least one previous abortion.

Sadly, there is a consequence to every action, and those having an abortion are no exception. There are two real areas of concern and consequences that someone considering an abortion will not hear from Pro-Choice, Planned Parenthood, or the ACLU. There is also an alternative to an abortion that one should seriously consider.

The Psychological Consequence

> After one's experience of Abortion, many can be guilt ridden, have anxiety, depression, experience a sense of loss, have hostility, entertain suicide and psychosis can set in. Any woman can suffer from not one but a combination of these problems. This trauma is recognized by the American Psychiatric Association as a psychological stress disorder and is listed in their Diagnostic and Statistical Manual of Mental Disorders.

> DSM III-R:309.89, Washington, D.C.,
> American Psychiatric Press,
> p. 250 , 1987.

The bottom line is that, irrespective of one's stance on abortion, the great majority of women having an abortion will experience symptoms of Post-Traumatic Stress Disorder (PTSD) in one form or another. This is particularly true for women approaching their thirties, forties, and fifties, who had abortions when they were young teenagers and in their early twenties. Many who were advocates of abortion in their youth have expressed significant remorse as they have matured in age. In many cases, the outward expression of guilt did not surface until years after the procedure took place—in a number of cases, more than ten years after the abortion.

Women have also experienced a number of PTSD symptoms, including depression, anger, impacted grief, chronic guilt, anxiety, intrusive memories, self-destructive behaviors, eating disorders, substance abuse, sexual maladjustment, and personality disorders, to name a few. Some abortion reactions may fit into a model of complicated bereavement or pathological grief.[nn]

The following is a more common example of PTSD showing up many years after person has had an abortion. Taken from the *Butler C. Journal of Family Practices 1996; 43:396-401*:

> Sally, aged 38, called her general practitioner (GP) to her home, because she was suffering from perineal bleeding. She had never presented with psychological problems. The GP noted that her apartment was remarkable for the number of soft toys that occupied every available space.

> When the GP asked Sally routine gynecological questions, Sally burst into tears and said she had 'never been happy' since she 'lost' her son. It emerged that, when she was 19, unemployed and still living with her parents, she had become pregnant. Her parents insisted that she have no further contact with the father and that she have a termination. After only a

brief chat with the doctor, she had a termination, although she felt that she was never asked what she really wanted.

Sally had vivid recollections of the procedure and commented that a 'profile' nurse told her that she had killed a perfectly formed little boy. She later married, but did not have children. She said that not a day goes by when she does not cry for her son. This was the first time that she had told anyone, apart from her husband, about her suffering.

Freedom of choice that subjects the individual to psychological bondage is not freedom.

Jesus said in Matthew 11: 28-29 (NIV):

Come to me, all you who are weary and burdened, and I will give you rest. Take my yoke upon you and learn from me, for I am gentle and humble in heart, and you will find rest for your souls. For my yoke is easy and my burden is light.

To those who have had an abortion, this may be an oversimplification of what you may be going through. Please take heart, Jesus really loves you and stands there with open arms, ready to forgive and give you rest. For those contemplating having an abortion, there is a way out that is biblical and will cause you less pain in the long run, which I will outline later in this chapter.

The Physical Consequence

> The public is misled into believing that legal abortion is a trivial incident, even a lunch hour procedure. There has been almost a conspiracy of silence in declaring its risks. This is medically indefensible when patients suffer as a result.

> *LAW ABORTION:*
> *A CRITICAL ASSESSMENT OF ITS RISKS,*
> Stallworthy pp.1245-1249

There are three main physical areas of concern for those contemplating an abortion, one of which is heavily debated by medical experts who seem to be rather biased when the opinion is from a pro-life or pro-choice advocate. However, numerous studies suggest that the three common medical risks associated with an abortion include breast cancer, future pre-term birth, and placenta previa.

Breast Cancer: It is a well-known and documented scientific fact that completing a full-term pregnancy provides the mother with a level of breast cancer protection. This is called "The Protective Effect."[oo] During an abortion, "The Protective Effect" is lost, resulting in an inverse effect that actually increases the risk of breast cancer. Research indicates that this risk is increased between thirty percent and one hundred percent over the life of the woman.[pp]

Future Risk of Pre-Term Birth: "A significant association was found between past abortion and the overall number of complications in the second half of pregnancy requiring medical intervention and/or admission to hospital, impending pre-term birth requiring betamimetics, pre-term birth, retention of the placenta, birth weight below 2000 g, light-for-dates infants in case of pre-term birth or birth

weight below 2000 g, and hyperbilirubinemia in infants with
birth weight below 2000 g."[qq]

Future Risk of Placenta Previa: Placenta (pluh-sen-tuh)
previa (pree-v-uh) means "placenta first." It occurs when the
placenta grows in the bottom of the uterus (womb) instead
of the top. The birth canal may be partly or totally blocked
by the placenta. It may be a very serious problem for both
mother and baby.[rr] At www.pubmed.gov, there are a number
of studies that indicate that an induced first trimester abortion
is a significant factor predisposing to placenta previa.

The Bottom Line on Abortion:

When it comes down to it, there are significant psychological and physicals risks associated with an abortion, which
the ACLU and Planned Parenthood do not disclose or discuss.
The ACLU considers the fetus as "stuff" rather than a life
worth considering. This is in line with its secular viewpoint
that humanity, morality, and consequence are relative to the
individual. Thus, the human being is nothing more than an
animal, a complicated composition of biochemistry—stuff.

> In June, 1977, the Louisiana ACLU affiliate
> offered an abortion at its annual fund-raising
> auction. The price was $30. The state director
> of the affiliate, Marlen Roeder, said that she
> was surprised by the critical reaction to the
> abortion auction: "Abortions, after all, are
> legal, and it's as legitimate, in my perspec-
> tive, for a women to get an abortion as it is for
> someone to get a divorce or to bid on a legal
> defense for a D.W.I. [driving while intoxi-
> cated] or any of the other professional services
> we offer."[ss]

On the other hand, in 2004, Planned Parenthood earned an estimated one hundred and four million dollars from its surgical abortion business alone[n], which begs the question: Why would they be motivated to provide alternatives to abortion when it would negatively impact their bottom line?

What Is the Alternative?

Consider the following: During the time before Moses was born, the Egyptian Pharaoh and his leaders were aware of a pending prophet and deliverer among the Hebrews. Therefore, Pharaoh declared that all Hebrew children born would be thrown into the Nile. The Pharaoh was literally considered a god to the Egyptian people. Thus, failure to obey his edicts usually had dire consequences to the guilty person and his or her family.

> Now a man of the house of Levi married a Levite woman, and she became pregnant and gave birth to a son. When she saw that he was a fine child, she hid him for three months. But, when she could hide him no longer, she got a papyrus basket for him and coated it with tar and pitch. Then she placed the child in it and put it among the reeds along the bank of the Nile. His sister stood at a distance to see what would happen to him.
>
> Then, Pharaoh's daughter went down to the Nile to bathe, and her attendants were walking along the river bank. She saw the basket among the reeds and sent her slave girl to get it. She opened it and saw the baby. He was crying, and she felt sorry for him.
>
> Exodus 2:1-6 (NIV)

There are a number of key lessons to consider before having an abortion that is derived from the Old Testament story of Moses:

1) The mother of Moses could have done a number of things to reduce the risks of having a baby during a time when the penalty for disobeying Pharaoh's orders by concealing the baby was execution. Abortion was not a medical option at the time. The mother could have concealed her pregnancy until birth then smothered the child to prevent it from suffering by being tossed into the Nile River. She would then have been one of the many that just gave up the child to protect her own life and the lives of her husband and existing children. Her decision would have been logical and appropriate given the alternatives and even encouraged by family members and close friends. Instead, the mother of Moses chose a different and more difficult path.

2) There was a point where the child could not be concealed any longer. The risk was too high for Moses' entire family for them to continue down this path of deception. Today, there are many women that feel the same way when their unwanted pregnancy is first realized. To go the distance would represent significant changes in their lives, add unplanned risk, or result in major personal disappointments with family and friends. The least risk solution is at the forefront, with many consequences conveniently concealed, including life-long emotional and potential physical baggage.

3) At this point, Moses' mother realized that she could not keep the baby. There are many women

throughout this country that feel the same way for whatever reason. They know that they cannot take care of a child at this particular point in their lives. However, what Moses' mother did was remarkable and represented a godly way out. She was willing to give up the child by entrusting God to find her newborn baby a home that was safe and secure.

Albeit simplistic, that is the key solution a woman should seriously consider before proceeding with an abortion. I have a good friend and colleague that provided consulting services to a "Quick Lube" business that I own in Winchester, Virginia. This friend is very successful, grounded, and married with children of his own. He is also an adopted child. During a number of talks I have had with him, my friend once stated: "If I was to ever meet my birth mother, I would thank her for not aborting me and for giving me a chance to live the life I now have." There was no resentment, no hurt, but an understanding that a long time ago his mother chose to give up a child for adoption rather than to have him removed from existence. That is a good choice with which God would be pleased.

Consider one other important positive consequence from the story of Moses. As a result of his mother's actions, a child was born that would later deliver approximately one million Hebrews from the bondage of slavery. Consider what God could do for your child if you give your child the opportunity to live.

And whoever welcomes a little child like this
in my name welcomes me [Jesus].
                              Matthew 18:5 (NIV)

The Fruitless Deeds of Sexual Deviancy

> The wrath of God is being revealed from heaven against all the godlessness and wickedness of men who suppress the truth by their wickedness, since what may be known about God is plain to them, because God has made it plain to them. For, since the creation of the world, God's invisible qualities — his eternal power and divine nature — have been clearly seen, being understood from what has been made, so that men are without excuse.
>
> For, although they knew God, they neither glorified him as God nor gave thanks to him, but their thinking became futile and their foolish hearts were darkened. Although they claimed to be wise, they became fools and exchanged the glory of the immortal God for images made to look like mortal man and birds and animals and reptiles.
>
> **Therefore, God gave them over in the sinful desires of their hearts to sexual impurity for the degrading of their bodies with one another.**
>
> Romans 1:18-24 (NIV)

Sadly, this is exactly the state that this country is in today. The path this country has taken has resulted in a progressive alienation and betrayal to God. Over the past eighty years, we have pushed our moral belief systems aside to embrace lies and deviant behaviors that have resulted in a society that is hostile to God.

We have bought into the greatest lie of the century and "exchanged the glory of the immortal God for images made to look like mortal man and birds and animals and reptiles" in an attempt to justify our existence through evolutionary theory. From a political policy standpoint, we are further alienating our society from all aspects of God via the so-called Separation Clause. By doing so, we are systematically forbidding our children, our government, and its people from connecting with God within the public venue.

We are living in a day where homosexuality, pornography, and other forms of sexual deviancy are now embraced in the name of "alternative lifestyles" and tolerance. Furthermore, any moral objections to these lifestyles are jeered through the media, the entertainment world, and political circles as homophobic and non-mainstream bigotry, while sexual promiscuity is heralded.

Case in point:

What is wrong with this country when a homosexual adulterous affair by the former New Jersey governor, James McGreevy, is cheered nationally within political and media circles as a "coming out of the closet" celebration?

Unknowingly, the acceptance of these lifestyles is the consequence of sin according to the Bible as evidence of God's hand being withdrawn from a wicked society. In this stage, God has therefore given us over to our sinful desires and to sexual impurities for the degrading of our bodies as this great nation and its people head full-steam toward God's ultimate judgment.

The picture here is rather straightforward from God's standpoint when considering the phrase **"given us over to our sinful desires."** To illustrate this, imagine a person hell-bent on doing something that is destructive to his body—say jumping out of a plane without a parachute. God is there holding the person back by trying to influence the person's reason, explaining the consequences, and blocking the way to the exit. Yet the person does not even acknowledge God's intervention, denies His existence, and is determined to venture out of the aircraft by any available means.

Eventually God steps aside and allows the inevitable. The end result is evident and predictable. If this person jumps out of the plane without a parachute, he may feel the exhilarating rush of the free-fall, but the end result will be personal destruction.

Now take this same scenario and use the United States as an example. As a nation, the more we push God out of the picture, the more we reap the results of sin and iniquity. National policy that attempts to redefine sin as a societal norm may appear to be unobtrusive, politically correct, tolerant, not affecting you or your family, benign, or even beneficial from a rationalization standpoint. Yet the consequence is ultimately another level of wickedness that God defines as an abomination. Committing and condoning these acts of sexual deviancy and these lifestyles only further alienates God from this nation as He withdraws His hand of protection.

There are three important causes and effects within the aforementioned Scripture that apply to people within this country and throughout the world:

1) God has made it clear that He has existed since the creation of the world and that His creative power is evident within the complexities of nature. Failing to recognize this truth results in an evolutionary mindset which has been disproved, but is still being touted as the answer to how the universe, earth, and mankind came into existence. This takes God out of the picture when there is so much evidence contrary to evolutionary theory. The Bible is therefore true when it states that, "Although they

claimed to be wise, they became fools." The impor- tant consequence of denying God's role in our creation is that we, as a nation, end up dishonoring our Maker while robbing Him of His glory. This is also identified as a great wickedness in the eyes of God. This wickedness eventually encompasses a standard of learning disseminated throughout our schools, which is changing the mindset of our future generations and leaders.

2) In this wicked state, God "gives us over to our sinful desires," thus allowing this generation to fall deeper into sexual impurity to include the degrading of our bodies. We then become increasingly wicked as each new generation is carried forward. This is our reward when we choose to alienate God from our lives and our society. During this death spiral, His divine protection becomes increasingly absent as we systematically push our protector, the God of the universe, aside from our daily lives.

3) The end result is a progressively wicked culture awaiting God's judgment—a culture described in Luke 17:28-29 (NIV): "It was the same in the days of Lot. People were eating and drinking, buying and selling, planting and building. But the day Lot left Sodom, fire and sulfur rained down from heaven and destroyed them all."

It is revealing and compelling that the two times Jesus was asked what the conditions of the world would be like during his second coming (the end times), he responded that it would be like the days of Noah and Lot. During both times, wickedness and sexual deviancy were paramount and universal. In the case of Noah, wickedness and sexual devi- ancy were on a global scale. In the case of Lot, they were on a micro scale, relating to the wicked cities of Sodom and

Gomorrah. In both cases, when the faithful objected to this deviancy, the result was ridicule or persecution, as is occurring today within this country. Today, there are gay action groups who protest in front of churches throughout America to influence or intimidate those who reject their lifestyles as a societal norm—as recently occurred in a Baptist church in Northern Virginia.

Yet, as with the cases of Noah and Lot, God's judgments were exacted upon the children of disobedience.[uu] There is strong evidence that God's judgment is being exacted upon the United States as we further abandon all forms of morality, while embracing every form of sexual wickedness.

The four main areas of sexual deviancy plaguing this country include: pornography, alternative lifestyles, pedophilia, and sexual promiscuity.

PORNOGRAPHY

Pornography within this country is a twelve billion dollar industry, currently outpacing revenues for all of the known main professional sports combined—including football, hockey, baseball, and basketball.[vv] It is too easily available from within our homes via pay-per-view, the Internet, and adult entertainment being offered within the privacy of hotel rooms. Call it adult entertainment, but in reality it is the exploitation and devaluation of the sexes that God considers holy. Furthermore, pornography is very addicting and is the root cause of most forms of sexual crimes, murder, and individual deviancy. It is also one of the fastest growing root causes for marital strife resulting in separation and divorce.

Contrary to most beliefs (mostly from the porn industry and the ACLU), pornography is not a victimless lifestyle. The following are examples of some of the most heinous crimes, which have been attributed to hardcore pornography via the perpetrators' own testimonies and by evidence from investigating officials.

Gary Bishop, Serial Killer
Ted Bundy, Serial Killer
Jeffrey Dahmer, Serial Killer
Klebold and Harris, Columbine Murderers[ww]

Is pornography addictive? The answer is absolutely yes. There are four stages associated with pornography addiction, which include:[xx]

1) **Addiction** – The addiction effect causes a porn-consumer to get hooked once involved with pornographic materials. At this stage, the consumer wants more and more. The pornographic materials provide a very powerful sexual stimulant or aphrodisiac effect, followed by sexual release, most often through masturbation.

2) **Escalation** – With the passage of time, the addicted porn-consumer needs rougher, more explicit, and in most cases, more "kinky" kinds of sexual material to get the same degree of sexual release as in the first stage.

3) **Desensitization** – Pornographic material which was originally perceived as shocking, taboo-breaking, illegal, repulsive and/or immoral, though still sexually arousing, in time has come to be seen as acceptable and commonplace to the user. The sexual activity depicted in the pornographic material becomes legitimized within the mind of the consumer.

4) **Acting out Sexually** – Within this forth stage, there is an increased tendency to act out sexually the behaviors viewed within the pornographic materials. This behavior frequently grows into a sexual addiction,

from which the consumer finds him or herself unable to modify or escape. This sexual addiction becomes an overpowering force preying upon the afflicted person, who can no longer break free regardless of the adverse consequences to his or her life.

How significant a problem is pornography within the US? Please note the following statistics taken from www. Familysafemedia.com and then reconsider just how victimless pornography is as a lifestyle: [yy]

- Average age of first Internet exposure to pornography? **11 years old**
- Largest consumer of Internet pornography? **12-17 age group**
- Fifteen- to seventeen-year-olds having multiple hardcore exposures? **80%**
- Eight- to sixteen-year-old having viewed pornography? **90% (most while doing homework)**
- Children's characters linked to thousands of porn sites? **26 (including Pokeman and Action Man)**
- US adults who regularly visit Internet pornography websites? **40 million**
- Promise Keeper's men who viewed pornography in last week? **53%**[zz]
- Christians who said pornography is a major problem in the home? **47%**
- Adults admitting to Internet sexual addiction? **10%**
- One of three visitors to all adult websites are women.

The plague of pornography traverses all ages and impacts all demographics, including the churches of believers. This is a very big problem that is basically being ignored by the public and aggressively defended by the ACLU under the guise of "freedom of speech."

Notwithstanding the tremendous harm that pornography causes, the ACLU Policy number 4 defends all forms of pornography, including child porn, as "free speech."

ALTERNATIVE LIFESTYLES

> Do you not know that the **wicked will not inherit the kingdom of God? Do not be deceived. Neither the sexually immoral nor idolaters nor adulterers nor male prostitutes nor homosexual offenders** nor thieves nor the greedy nor drunkards nor slanderers nor swindlers will inherit the kingdom of God.
>
> 1 Corinthians 6:8-10

Before I get too deep within this section, I want to make it very clear that sin is a universal consequence of our alienation from God. Sexual deviancy is a consequence of God's withdrawal from our society as indicated within Romans 1:24. The wickedness mentioned within 1 Corinthians 6:8-10 includes all forms of sexual immorality, such as pornography, fornication, adultery, pedophilia, polygamy, bestiality, and homosexuality.

However, before one considers attacking the homosexual community, one must also realize that the list mentioned above includes heterosexuals as well. The bottom line is that sexual deviancy will not be tolerated by God, irrespective of what some forward-thinking churches are endorsing. The judgment seat of God will hold all accountable for their actions irrespective of the endorsements of the ACLU, liberal judges, politicians, corporations, and some forward thinking churches. Those churches and leaders defending these lifestyles are the very persons that the Bible warns as being the "blind leaders of the blind," where both will end up in divine judgment.[aaa] We are also warned to stay away from them.

There are no alternative lifestyles acceptable to God. There are no marriages other than that between a man and woman. If you have embraced a position that alternative lifestyles are an acceptable norm within our society, then you have unknowingly taken a position against God by compromising His Word. Furthermore, you will be held accountable for this position when we all stand before God in judgment.

> Woe to those who call evil good and good evil, who put darkness for light and light for darkness, who put bitter for sweet and sweet for bitter.
>
> Isaiah 5:20 (NIV)

PEDOPHILIA

Pedophilia is becoming an epidemic within this country and is victimizing the very innocent and defenseless children that we as a country have sworn to defend as defined within our Constitution. When performing a search within the National Alert Registry, I was surprised to find that forty registered sex offenders resided within the small community in which I work. This is rather disturbing considering that this community has a large Evangelical Christian community base. When searching other most sought after communities within Loudoun County and Northern Virginia, the search count was much higher. The reality is that within every community there are sex offenders living among us.

The following are some facts regarding the consumer demand for this deviant lifestyle.

- Daily Gnutella requests for child pornography? **116,000/day**
- Web sites offering illegal child pornography? **100,000+**

- Sexual solicitations of youth made in chat rooms? **89%**
- Youths who receive sexual solicitations? **20%**

As a child, I was brought up in Chelsea, Massachusetts, a small city just north of Boston. At age ten, I would get on the bus to the inner city to buy old coins, hockey sticks, baseballs, and other sports equipment at "Larry's Leftovers." I would hang out with my friends and play sports at Prattville or Voke Park. In all my youth, I never feared being abducted or assaulted by a pedophile. Today, most families are afraid to have their children wander beyond their street or within shouting distance from their home. What has changed in thirty-five years?

Thirty five years ago, there were red-light districts that harbored the indecencies we readily see available within the pay-per-view channels inside our home or over the Internet. These districts were normally located within large metropolitan cities in the so-called red zones. Even within these districts, the push by local activists in coordination with local police and other political officials was constantly working toward cleaning up these areas or at least keeping them under control. During this time, alternative lifestyles were unheard of within mainstream America and were deemed unacceptable within our society. Yet behind the scenes of the '70s, a storm was brewing.

> Unfortunately, gaining access to children has been a long-term goal of the homosexual movement. In 1972, the National Coalition of Gay Organizations adopted a "Gay Rights Platform" that included the following demand: "Repeal of all laws governing the age of sexual consent." David Thorstad, a spokesman for the homosexual rights movement and NAMBLA (North American Man/Boy Love Association),

clearly states the objectives:" The ultimate goal of the gay liberation movement is the achievement of sexual freedom for all - not just equal rights for lesbians and gay men, but also freedom of sexual expression for young people and children." This goal has not changed since it was articulated in 1972.[bbb]

It is no wonder that NAMBLA can be found present among the majority of the Gay Pride celebrations and marches. The ACLU and the gay community would like you to believe that child pornography and other forms of child exploitation are victimless crimes, yet the evidence heavily refutes this.

In a recent *CNN* article concerning Attorney General Gonzales:

> The Attorney General said one of every five children online is now solicited. He cited a recent estimate that 50,000 predators are online at any given time prowling for children.

> "It is graphic, but if we do not talk candidly, then it is easy for people to turn away," he said." I have seen pictures of older men forcing naked young girls to have anal sex," Gonzales said. "There are videos on the Internet of very young daughters forced to have intercourse and oral sex with their fathers.

> "Viewing this was shocking and it makes my stomach turn, but while these descriptions may make some uncomfortable, we will not defeat this threat unless we all really understand the nature of the child pornography now prevalent

on the Internet," he said. Gonzales said the public must not consider child porn a victimless crime.

"There are images of graphic sexual and physical abuse of innocent children, even babies," he said. "It is brutal; it is heinous, and it is criminal."

The plague of pedophilia extends to the homosexual and heterosexual community as well, with a significant portion of cases that are a result of incest or abuse from a friend close to the family. Remember that God said that he would "give us over to our sinful desires" to any nation that turns their back on Him. Well, this is just another example of the sexual deviancy mentioned in this warning. The bottom line is that we subject ourselves to multiple forms of sexual deviancy, including pedophilia, as we further push God out of our society.

Isn't that exactly what this country did in 1947, when our Supreme Court declared that the "Walls of separation between church and state need to be high and impregnable?" We threw God out of our schools in 1961 and have been systematically removing him from the public venue ever since. It is no wonder that we are presently reaping the sins of our past national policy mistakes concerning God. The movements and coalitions being formed today that represent incomprehensible deviancy are a result of God's withdrawal from a nation and targeting it for divine judgment.

When God rose King Nebuchadnezzar and the Babylonians up to destroy Israel, the root cause of Israel's destruction was not this vast military force. The underlying issue was Israel's abandonment of God's principals coupled with the acceptance of Baal and other forms of idol worship. One popular form of worship was normally celebrated to the gods of fertility through sexual encounters with the temple prostitutes of Baal.

Let's just say that Baal worship was booming in Israel during this time. King Nebuchadnezzar was only the tool God used to exact his judgment on a sinful nation.

Likewise, we as a country have bastardized our "freedom of speech" clause within our Constitution to accept all forms of sexual deviancy and lifestyles, while closing all doors for morality in the name of the "separation of church and state." On one hand, this nation has accepted this deviancy as a norm within our society, while rejecting all forms of moral decency and controls based upon Godly principles. Is it no wonder that our mortal enemies across this world are increasing daily with new enemies rising within our own hemisphere. Could it be that the rise of Al Qaeda and the war on terrorism is the beginning of the end of this country? Our southern borders and our domestic unrest are further warnings that need to be heeded. Remember that the Roman Empire, although formidable and expansive, was defeated by the barbarians who burned Rome to the ground.

Yet, through all of this secular hogwash about the rights of sexual expression, let it be known that God's position on pedophilia is crystal clear:

> But if anyone causes one of these little ones who believe in me to sin, it would be better for him to have a large millstone hung around his neck and to be drowned in the depths of the sea.
>
> Matthew 18:6 (NIV)

These were one to two-ton millstones. This is a very strong and graphic image of how God views those who exploit children. Let there be no doubt that anyone who lives a life that victimizes the innocent will be punished, irrespective of efforts of the ACLU and other groups to change public policy on the age of consent.

SEXUAL PROMISCUITY:

> There's more to sex than mere skin on skin.
> Sex is as much spiritual mystery as physical
> fact. As written in Scripture, "The two become
> one." Since we want to become spiritually
> one with the Master, we must not pursue the
> kind of sex that avoids commitment and inti-
> macy, leaving us lonelier than ever—the kind
> of sex that can never "become one." There is
> a sense in which sexual sins are different from
> all others. In sexual sin, we violate the sacred-
> ness of our own bodies, these bodies that were
> made for God-given and God-modeled love,
> for "becoming one" with another. Or didn't
> you realize that your body is a sacred place,
> the place of the Holy Spirit? Don't you see
> that you can't live however you please, squan-
> dering what God paid such a high price for?
> The physical part of you is not some piece of
> property belonging to the spiritual part of you.
> God owns the whole works. So let people see
> God in and through your body.
>
> I Corinthians 6:16-20 (Message)

According to the American Academy of Pediatrics, 36.9 percent of fourteen-year-olds have had sex, which is more than one out of three. Among twelfth graders, 66.4 percent have had sex.[ccc]

Among teens, each year there are about three million cases of sexually transmitted diseases (STDs) and approximately one million pregnancies. Human immunodeficiency virus (HIV) infection is the sixth leading cause of death among persons aged fifteen to twenty-four in the United States.[ddd]

Yet the ACLU has launched a drive to persuade education officials in eighteen states to reject Federal government-affiliated abstinence programs. According to *The Washington Times*, the ACLU, citing data from a December 2004 report by Rep. Henry Waxman, D-Calif., claims that the programs discriminate against homosexuals, contain too much religious connotation, and spread false information.[eee]

The ACLU actively supports all forms of sexual freedoms, irrespective of age, gender preference, and act. The ACLU is more interested in passing out condoms and birth control pills than in educating the masses to wait until marriage before having sex. Couple that policy viewpoint with the world bombarded with pornography, alternative lifestyle tolerance, and other forms of sexual deviancy as an acceptable norm, is it any wonder why our youths are engaging in sex at a very young age? This wicked lifestyle is further carried forward as they grow into adults and contributes to extramarital affairs when they finally settle down into marriage.

The bottom line is that God did not intend us to be sexually promiscuous. Sex was intended to be an expression of love and procreation between a man and a woman through the sacred vow of marriage. It was intended to join the souls of two beings into one.

> For this reason, a man will leave his father and mother and be united to his wife, and they will become one flesh.
> Genesis 2:24 (NIV)

However, when promiscuity is the norm, we are joining our souls with those with whom we are promiscuous.

> Do you not know that he who unites himself
> with a prostitute is one with her in body? For
> it is said, "The two will become one flesh."
>
> 1 Corinthians 6:16 (NIV)

To the believer in Christ, this is a defilement of what God calls the temple of the Holy Spirit. To the unbeliever, you create a sanctum of wickedness within your spirit as your heart grows callous to what is morally right. Let's now add the mindset of the secular humanist, where right and wrong are irrelevant. We have many within this country heading down a path to the destruction about which Jesus warned us.

> Enter through the narrow gate. For wide is
> the gate and broad is the road that leads to
> destruction, and many enter through it.
>
> Matthew 7:13 (NIV)

The course to the kingdom of God has always been the straight and narrow path, with the compass being God's Word from the teachings of the Bible. Any alternative course represents the wide path that the Bible sternly warns all persons venturing within it to avoid.

If you are reading this with a self-realization that you have been traveling on the road to destruction, there is hope. God's grace can place you back on the straight and narrow path to His Kingdom if you abandon your current path, repent, and follow after the truth from the saving grace of Jesus Christ.

To those of you who are considering this for the first time, you must understand the divine transformations that a Christian goes through for this to make sense. It is this transformation that can deliver you from these sins. When a person asks Jesus into their life with a sincere heart, two major transformations take place.

> For it is by grace you have been saved, **through faith** and this not from yourselves, it is the gift of God.
>
> Ephesians 2:8 (NIV)

1. **Salvation:** As mentioned earlier, we cannot save ourselves according to our own merit, and each person alive has fallen short of the glory of God. Yet, for those who believe that Jesus is the only way to salvation and have asked Him into their life, then salvation is returned from God as a free gift according to your faith.

> Do not conform any longer to the pattern of this world, but be transformed by the renewing of your mind. Then you will be able to test and approve what God's will is—his good, pleasing and perfect will.
>
> Romans 12:2 (NIV)

2. **Our Mind and Belief System:** As we draw close to God's Word, our understanding and belief system will change as the Holy Spirit teaches us and transforms our hearts to align with the will of God. When this happens, we become more acutely aware of and distant from the sins that may have had an influence to our lives. In many cases, the Holy Sprit begins to deliver us from lifestyles that are either immoral or harmful such as drug abuse, alcoholism, sexual addiction, rage, etc.

The end result is a lifestyle that is at peace with God and aligned to His will. This is how we connect with God. The ultimate purpose of this chapter is not to condemn the person on the path to destruction. It is, however, a humble plea and warning to communicate to those venturing in sin that there is still hope, irrespective of your circumstances. Jesus stated very clearly His heart's desire for the lost when the Pharisees complained bitterly that He was associating himself with and seeking out the sinners of His day.

> When the Pharisees saw this, they asked his disciples, "Why does your teacher eat with tax collectors and 'sinners'?"
>
> Matthew 9:11-13 (NIV)

Important Note: During Jesus' time, Israel was occupied by the Roman Empire. Jews were selected by the Romans to collect taxes and were despised by their countrymen. They were considered traitors and were hated by all.

> On hearing this, Jesus said, "It is not the healthy who need a doctor, but the sick. But go and learn what this means: 'I desire mercy, not sacrifice. For I have not come to call the righteous, but sinners.'"

Likewise, is it my prayerful desire that if you are a victim of Satan's lies and living a lifestyle deserving judgment, I humbly implore you to consider an alternative course and submit yourself at the mercy seat of the cross. Confess your sins to Jesus, ask for His forgiveness, and ask Him to help you change the direction of your life. The next step would be to drive a stake in the ground with determination to abandon the past and seek after Jesus through His Word and prayer, and by fellowship with other men and women of faith that can help hold you accountable.

> The night is nearly over; the day is almost here.
> **So let us put aside the deeds of darkness**

and put on the armor of light. Let us behave decently, as in the daytime, not in orgies and drunkenness, not in sexual immorality and debauchery, not in dissension and jealousy. **Rather, clothe yourselves with the Lord Jesus Christ, and do not think about how to gratify the desires of the sinful nature.**

Romans 13:12-14 (NIV)

There Is a Consequence to Our Nation's Actions

Does God pervert justice? Does the Almighty pervert what is right? When your children sinned against him, **he gave them over to the penalty of their sin.**

Job 8:3-4 (NIV)

For the <u>wages of sin is death</u>, but the gift of God is eternal life in Christ Jesus our Lord.

Romans 6:23 (NIV)

The Choice

You are free to choose between two masters, but you are not free to adjust the consequences of your choice. Each of the two masters pays with his own kind of currency. The currency of sin is death. That is all you can expect or hope for in life without God. Christ's currency is eternal life—new life with God that begins on earth and continues forever with God. [fff]

The same principle applies to a nation as well as its people. When a country chooses to embrace sin while shunning the moral teachings of God, the wages earned and received by that nation will result in is its eventual ruin and death. Likewise, when a person embraces sin as a matter of personal choice, they will reap the consequences of that lifestyle. Therefore, it is important for readers of this book to evaluate the choices they have made with their lives, family, and community.

Secondly, readers should carefully consider the decisions that they will make so as to provide for and protect the ones they love. If you know in advance that a robber is going to break into your home, what steps would you take to protect your family? If the wages of sin is death (eternal separation from God) and you understand the character of Satan (your enemy), what would you be willing to do as both an individual and as united churches of believers to make a difference? In the Bible, Jesus clearly states that "the thief comes only to steal and kill and destroy; I have come that they may have life, and have it to the fullest."[ggg]

When we turn our back on God, the consequence of that decision allows Satan to rob, kill, and destroy us individually and as a society. Satan does that by allowing us to adopt a belief system such as evolution that questions God's existence. By accepting lies that force us to establish laws that push God out of our government, schools, and the public venue; by ignoring the cries of the unborn; and by devaluing the sanctity of marriage to embrace alternative lifestyles and all other forms of sexual deviancy. In the end, the nation that has embraced sin becomes so corrupt that God intervenes by exacting his judgment, as He did thousand of years ago with Israel.

As mentioned earlier, the Old Testament books of 1-Kings, 2-Kings, 1-Chronicles and 2-Chronicles tell of a period of time when Israel began to turn away from the same God that delivered its people out of Egypt to the Promised Land.

A rebellious nation, Israel began to embrace idol worship, which included paying tribute to the temple prostitutes of Baal. During this time, king after king was identified within the Bible as being "more wicked" than his predecessor.

Occasionally, a godly king would rise to power and the nation of Israel would be at peace or would receive blessings from God in terms of prosperity, victory against enemies, or both. When a wicked leader would rise, the opposite would take place, as God would allow other nations to attack, defeat, and persecute Israel. Finally, King Manasseh was the straw that broke the camel's back.

During King Manasseh's reign, great sin and wickedness was so rampant within Israel that God could not differentiate between them and their enemies.

> Manasseh, King of Judah, has committed these abominations, and has done things more wicked than all that the Amorites did, who were before him, and has made Judah also to sin with his idols; [12] therefore thus says the LORD, the God of Israel, Behold, I am bringing upon Jerusalem and Judah such evil that the ears of every one who hears of it will tingle. [13] **And I will stretch over Jerusalem the measuring line of Samaria, and the plummet of the house of Ahab; and I will wipe Jerusalem as one wipes a dish, wiping it and turning it upside down.**
>
> 2 Kings 21:11-13 (NIV)

In the United States of America, our society is becoming increasingly more rebellious toward God. Each generation is worse than the preceding one. It is no wonder that this nation is systematically being torn apart from within and without. This falling away is exacerbated by the liberal elitists within this country who are quick to promote their immoral actions and policies. It is their pride and source of strength to brainwash present and future generations. Meanwhile, the conservatives who hold true to the moral teachings of God are being constantly assailed by the elitists as being out of touch with mainstream America.

The Pride of this Country Will Result in Its Destruction if We Do Not Heed the Warnings

> **Such is the destiny of all who forget God;**
> so perishes the hope of the godless. What he trusts in is fragile; what he relies on is a spider's web. He leans on his web, but it gives way; he clings to it, but it does not hold.
>
> Job 8:13-15 (NIV)

Any people that rely upon their own wisdom and source of strength while abandoning God are building their hope and future on a lie that will eventually fail them.

In the days of Moses, Egypt gave credit to their many idols and false gods as the source of their prosperity. They also relied upon their vast armies to enforce the edicts of Pharaoh. During that time, Pharaoh and his household were also considered gods to the people of Egypt and were served and worshipped accordingly.

The strength and governance of the Egyptians revolved heavily around polytheism and idol worship. This was their pride, source of confidence, and power. This was also the focal point of attack by which the Lord God used plagues to break down Egypt's defenses.

The following table illustrates a few examples of the plagues that God exacted on Egypt. The plagues were specifically targeted to its gods (their source of confidence), in whom the Egyptians put their trust.[hhh]

1) Hapi (also called Apis), the bull god, god of the Nile; Isis, goddess of the Nile; Khnum, ram god, guardian of the Nile; and others. In return, the Lord's first plague was to turn the Nile to blood (Exodus 7:14-25).
2) Heqet, a "frog-head" goddess of birth. In return, the Lord unleashed a plague of frogs (Exodus 8:1-15).
3) Hathor, goddess with a cow head; Apis the bull god, symbol of fertility. In return, the Lord sent the plague that killed the Egyptian livestock (Exodus 9:1-7).
4) Sekhmet, goddess with power over disease; Sunu, the pestilence god; Isis, goddess of healing. In return, God sent the plague of boils (Exodus 9:8-12).
5) Re, the sun god; Horus, a sun god; Nut, a sky goddess; Hathor, a sky goddess. In return, God laid a blanket of darkness over the skies of Egypt (Exodus 10:21-29).
6) Min, god of reproduction; Heqet, goddess who attended women at childbirth; Isis, goddess who protected children; Pharaoh's firstborn son, a god. In return, God sent the angel of death to kill the entire firstborn sons of Egypt (Exodus 11:1-12:30).
7) The vast armies of Egypt to enforce the will of the Pharaoh. In return, God drowned them in the Red Sea (Exodus 15:3-5).

These few examples provide a powerful lesson to any nation that abandons the Lord God, while relying on its own wisdom and pride as the source of self-governance—especially when the faithful are persecuted.

What Is the Pride and Strength of Our Country?

There are three major areas of strength within this country that were once all rooted in our relationship with God. Since we are abandoning God in these areas, they will also serve as the very source of our own judgment.

1. Our democratic system of governance
2. Our military and industrial base
3. Our geographic location

OUR DEMOCRATIC SYSTEM OF GOVERNANCE

The United States of America has always been a nation of laws that has taken pride in its Constitution and its democratic system of government. This democracy has been a beacon of light and a model to which other countries have aspired for years. However, the glue that has held this system of government together has always been its historical reliance and faith in God.

Unfortunately, "one nation under God" was replaced with the "Separation Clause." Therefore, it is this very same system of governance and pride that God is tearing apart from within. Our two-party political system is more interested in serving its party-line constituents than the American public. Our freedom of speech laws have been abused in such a manner by the liberal media that they take no thought in jeopardizing the lives of our military men and women in harm's way, while emboldening our enemies abroad. We have a growing list of judges that are legislating from the bench instead of enforcing the laws that they were appointed or elected to uphold. When tasked to defend the innocent, they are making decisions based upon their own personal views instead of the prevailing and established laws. All this is happening as our leaders are too busy slinging mud at each other instead of providing strong leadership for the American people by defending the Constitution which they have sworn to protect. The reality is that our democratic system is imploding as a result of our moral decay.

OUR MILITARY

As a retired military officer with over twenty-five years of service, I take great pride in our servicemen and women. We have been blessed as a country by our military's ability to reach out and touch our enemies anytime and anywhere in the world. For years, this has been a great deterrent for any nation that wanted to mess with us. It is with great sadness, therefore, that I fear for our nation's armed forces as I watch God being slowly kicked out of and further regulated within our military installations both here and abroad. This is being done by the litigious nature of the ACLU under the banner of the "Separation Clause." Unfortunately, there is a new trend whereby senior officers are trying to be politically correct in an effort to avoid offending anyone rather than to do what is right for their troops. The end result has been a series of poor military leadership decisions to restrict the ability of chaplains to proclaim the Word of God as they were ordained to perform. The very last thing this country wants to mess around with is God's divine protection of our troops. Yet that is exactly what is happening.

Throughout the history of the Bible, it has always been the military that has paid the price for the sins of its leaders. Some of the greatest military defeats within the Old Testament resulted when the people of Israel and their leaders disobeyed or abandoned God's guiding principles.

OUR GEOGRAPHIC LOCATION

For years, our geographic location has been a source of strength and protection. North America is flanked by two oceans: the Atlantic and the Pacific. We have also been friends with our neighbors in Canada and Mexico for years, whose borders are predominantly unguarded.

Our country has enjoyed a vast, fruitful land, rich in natural and human resources. Yet today we are seeing our internal resources, industrial base, land, and intellectual capital being squandered and outsourced to our potential enemies. We are also reaping the consequences of sin as our land is going through some of the worst weather patterns in history

We have been very blessed and at peace within the confines of our borders for years. Yet, on September 11, 2001, there occurred a brutal wakeup call that proved to the entire world how vulnerable we truly are. Unfortunately, after five years, the lessons learned from 9/11 have barely been heeded. Today there are politicians more interested in not offending people than in safeguarding our borders or profiling those most likely to commit terrorist acts within this country.

Thousands of years ago, King Nebuchadnezzar of ancient Babylon (modern-day Iraq) was raised to power by God to ultimately defeat Israel while subjecting the remnants of a once blessed and powerful nation to that of destruction, resettlement, and slavery. Today we have an equivalent scenario unfolding within this country:

1 As a nation, we are under attack from Al Qaeda and other Muslim extremists both at home and abroad. The events of 9/11 serve as only a warning of things to come. This country is too open and vulnerable for us not to get hit again. Furthermore, the political correctness policy of our government, exacerbated by the liberal left and the ACLU, greatly hinders us

from implementing safeguards within our country to protect our citizens, labeling many such efforts "racial profiling." Instead, we are searching eighty-year-old grandmothers at our airports while Homeland Security teaches a policy of self-preservation in case we get hit again. This is an example of God confusing the minds of our leaders into making poor policy decisions, which opens this country up to a future attack. Meanwhile, through our ongoing addiction to their oil supplies, we continue to finance the very nations that teach hatred of the United States.

2) We continue to pour billions of dollars of technology, intellectual capital, and money into China as it moves full speed toward modernizing its military, which is now considered a direct threat to the balance of power in East Asia. China is also one of the primary suppliers of military hardware and technology to Iran. Additionally, by bolstering China's economy, the United States is suffering in two major areas. First, our industrial base is being outsourced to a communist country that may use its production capabilities in a military capacity against us. Secondly, China is now a major consumer of oil, which is the primary reason that the American people are paying three dollars a gallon at the pumps during the time of this writing. We are basically financing a communist country's military and industrial base to the detriment of our own nation and future generations.

3) Iran and Syria are the primary contributors of weapons, training, and insurgent resources that are being used to attack our armed forces stationed in Iraq and Afghanistan. Iran has also made public its intention to continue its nuclear program and its desire to destroy Israel as it continues to pour

millions of dollars in weapons and funding into Syria and terrorist organizations such as Hezbollah. The United States is also depicted in Iran as the great Satan, who they believe will ultimately be defeated by Allah in some divine military victory.

4) We are being invaded by millions of illegal aliens from our southern borders. Most are looking for a better life for themselves and their families while many non-Mexicans are also finding their way into this country. One of the consequences of taking limited action to protect our borders has been the rise of the popular MS-13 gangs, which are infiltrating our inner cities. Furthermore, there is mounting evidence that many of these and other gang members are joining our military to learn the art of war so that they can become more effective killers within our own streets. This is just one example of the internal destruction awaiting us if we continue to turn a blind eye to this growing issue.

5) The Cuban alliance is growing within South America, as other nations are being brainwashed into believing that the United States is the new evil empire of the twenty-first century. For example, the distaste of President Chavez of Venezuela for the US has resulted in his alignment with Cuba and more recently with China, North Korea, Syria, and Iran. [iii]

6) The Bible states in Leviticus 18:28 that "if you defile the land, it will vomit you out as it vomited out the nations that were before you." This was in reference to the nation of Israel, when it came to obeying the moral teachings of God. It also applies to this nation. Do you think it is a coincidence that New Orleans, the center of Mardi Gras and sexual debauchery, would be ripped apart by Hurricane Katrina at this time in our history? Is it

a coincidence that Florida, which celebrates Gay Pride Day at Disney World and is the center of sexual promiscuity each spring break, is now the focal point of hurricane alley during an extreme period within our history? These are only the beginning. They should also serve as a warning to California, Massachusetts, and Nevada, which are major centers of sexual deviancy and promoters of alternative lifestyles.

It does not take a rocket scientist to read the writing on the wall. As a nation, we are reaping the consequences of our sin. As a people, we cannot be so naive as to think that God will not exact his judgment on a nation that turns its back on Him while embracing all other forms of sin. The more we push God out of the picture, the more this country will continue to spiral out of control and out of favor with Him.

> He who sows iniquity will reap calamity and futility, and the rod of his wrath [with which he smites others] will fail.
>   Proverbs 22:8 (Amplified Bible)

One of the consequences of a nation that sows iniquity is that it will reap calamity and ineffectiveness. Most importantly, a sinful nation will lose its victorious edge in battle and will eventually suffer defeat. So, before you blame the President, consider the state of our nation in terms of our moral compass.

> For he who sows to his own flesh (lower nature, sensuality) will from the flesh reap decay and ruin and destruction; but he who sows to the Spirit will from the Spirit reap eternal life.
>   Galatians 6:8 (Amplified Bible)

As I stated before, "the wages of sin is death." It is critical that the readers of this book know for whom and for what they are working. Irrespective of your personal stance or belief, what you sow is what you reap. Furthermore, inaction in response to sin, especially when you have the power to make a difference, is the equivalent of passive acceptance. In this case, you are taking a position and have made a personal choice of tolerance.

If you are like me, then you are tired of watching the bad guys win. You are tired of being told that you must refrain from mentioning God within the public circle when the "Ten Commandments" are mounted on the walls of the Supreme Court. This is a critical time in our history, a time when we should be embracing God instead of shunning him. Additionally, the churches are predominantly weak and very, very lukewarm.

> I know you inside and out and find little to
> my liking. You're not cold, you're not hot—
> far better to be either cold or hot! You're
> stale. You're stagnant. You make me want to
> vomit. You brag, 'I'm rich, I've got it made,
> I need nothing from anyone, oblivious that in
> fact you're a pitiful, blind beggar, threadbare
> and homeless.
> Revelation 3:15-17 (The Message)

Revelations 3:15-17 referred to the church of Laodicea. They were comfortable in their wealth and respected and happy in their size. Yet they lacked zeal and effectiveness for the kingdom of God. Therefore, God labeled this church lukewarm and warned that he would vomit them out of His mouth. A wicked nation will suffer a similar consequence, as the land will vomit its people out over time.

Many churches within this country have so much fear of losing their not-for-profit status that they are compromising the core teachings of the Bible while taking a very limited stance on defending the gospel. There are others that grow multimillion dollar "super churches" with thousands of followers, yet there is no unity of purpose among the believers toward putting God back into our country. Aside from saving the lost, which is the first and foremost objective, putting God back into our country should be our unified mission and priority for the sake of our future generations!

The enemies of the church are very vocal and determined. They are not going to go away until the churches of believers unite, stop the infighting, and focus upon turning this country toward a spirit of repentance and spiritual reunification.

Making Things
Right with God

When Minister Joe Wright was asked to open the new session of the Kansas State Senate in January, 1996, everyone was expecting the usual politically correct generalities, but this is what they heard:[iii]

The Prayer

"Heavenly Father, we come before You today to ask for Your forgiveness and seek Your direction and guidance. We know Your Word says "Woe to those who call evil good,"[kkk] but that is exactly what we have done. We have lost our spiritual equilibrium and reversed our values. We confess that:

- We have ridiculed the absolute truth of Your Word and called it pluralism.

- We have worshipped other gods and called it multiculturalism.

- We have endorsed perversion and called it alternative lifestyle.

- We have exploited the poor and called it the lottery.

- We have rewarded laziness and called it welfare.

- We have killed our unborn and called it choice.

- We have shot the abortionist and called it justifiable.

- We have neglected to discipline our children and called it building self-esteem.

- We have abused power and called it politics.

- We have coveted our neighbor's possessions and called it ambition.

- We have polluted the air with profanity and pornography and called it freedom of expression.

- We have ridiculed the time-honored values of our forefathers and called it enlightenment.

Search us, O God, and know our hearts today, try us and see if there is any wicked way in us, cleanse us from every sin, and set us free. Guide and bless these men and women who have been sent here by the people of Kansas and who have been ordained by You to govern this great state. Grant them Your wisdom to rule and may their decisions direct us to the center of Your will. I ask it in the name of your Son, the Living Savior, Jesus Christ, Amen."

The response was immediate. A number of legislators walked out during the prayer in protest. In six short weeks, Central Christian Church, where Rev. Wright is pastor, logged more than five thousand phone calls, of which only forty-seven responded negatively. The church is now receiving international requests for copies of this prayer from India, Africa, and Korea. Commentator Paul Harvey aired this prayer in his "The Rest of the Story" radio program. Not only did he receive a larger response to this program than any other he has ever aired, he has received more requests for reprints than any other article he has ever printed.

Minister Joe Wright was on the right track in his prayer to the Kansas Senate. Individually, we need to repent and take a personal position to follow after God and His principles without compromise to his word. To do this, we need to confess our sins, we need to ask for his forgiveness, we need to repent, we need to seek purposefully after God's will, and we need to read His Word for guidance and consistency of purpose.

I cannot state how important it is to read, meditate, and seek after God's Word through the Bible. For the past twenty-five years of being a Christian, I had never read the Bible from front to back until I began reading it four years ago. It is estimated that over ninety percent of all those who profess their faith in Jesus have never read the Bible from cover to cover. If you are like me, you probably tried to read the Bible from beginning to end but got bogged down in the Old Testament around the Book of Numbers. My suggestion to you is to purchase the *One Year Bible*, which will provide you with daily readings with sections from the Old and New Testament, Psalms, and Proverbs. In one year, you will have read the Bible from cover to cover using this method. It is amazing how the Holy Spirit will increase your understanding of the heartbeat of God if you determine within yourself to understand His Word.

Collectively, we need to put aside our denominational differences and unite as churches of believers against those trying to remove God from our society. Furthermore, we need to take a position to undo the mistakes of the past that have been imposed upon us by this secular humanistic mindset, which has infiltrated our schools, colleges, leaders, courts, and public policy.

> But you must remember, beloved, the predictions of the apostles of our Lord Jesus Christ. They said to you, "In the last time there will be scoffers, following their own ungodly passions." It is these who cause divisions, worldly people, devoid of the Spirit. But you, beloved, build yourselves up in your most holy faith; pray in the Holy Spirit; keep yourselves in the love of God, waiting for the mercy of our Lord Jesus Christ that leads to eternal life. And **have mercy on those who doubt; save others by snatching them out of the fire; to others show mercy with fear, hating even the garment stained by the flesh.**
>
> Jude 1:17-23 (NIV)

The bottom line in getting right with God is that it must start with you first. It is also a lifetime commitment. As mentioned in the beginning, you will serve one of two masters. You will either be a servant of God or a slave to sin. The latter may seem to be a lot of fun to the non-discerning, but the end result will only lead to death and divine judgment. By serving God, the wages you will earn will be life, love, joy, and the peace that surpasses all worldly understanding. The question is which will you choose?

> This day I call heaven and earth as witnesses against you that I have set before you life and

death, blessings and curses. Now choose life,
so that you and your children may live.

Deuteronomy 30:19 (NIV)

**If at any time I announce that a nation
or kingdom is to be uprooted, torn down
and destroyed, and if that nation I warned
repents of its evil, then I will relent and not
inflict on it the disaster I had planned.** And
if at another time I announce that a nation or
kingdom is to be built up and planted, and if
it does evil in my sight and does not obey me,
then I will reconsider the good I had intended
to do for it. "Now therefore say to the people
of Judah and those living in Jerusalem,
'This is what the LORD says: Look! **I am
preparing a disaster for you and devising
a plan against you. So turn from your evil
ways, each one of you, and reform your
ways and your actions.'**

Jeremiah 18:7-11 (NIV)

Putting God
Back in Our Nation

When I sat down on the bus that day, I had
no idea history was being made—I was only
thinking of getting home. But I had made
up my mind. After so many years of being a
victim of the mistreatment my people suffered,
not giving up my seat—and whatever I had
to face afterwards—was not important. I did
not feel any fear sitting there. I felt the Lord
would give me the strength to endure whatever I had to face. It was time for someone
to stand up—or in my case, sit down. So I
refused to move.

Rosa Parks (Civil Rights Activist)[III]

The average person knows that the path this country is on
is not the one each of us signed on for. We have been
led blindly down this path while being told by a very vocal
minority to suck it up and deal with it. At age forty-five, I am
tired of being pushed in the corner while I watch this great
nation head full steam toward God's divine judgment. When

God's judgment is exacted upon us, the fallout will take the good out along with the bad.

As a military officer, I was sworn to defend the Constitution of the United States of America from all enemies, both foreign and domestic. The Constitution was built on the principals of God by our God-fearing Founding Fathers. Yet today liberal judges take it upon themselves to legislate contrary to the will of the people, while those in authority do nothing to defend the constitution to which they swore their allegiance.

The goal of this book is to heighten your level of awareness of the lies that you have been fed since your childhood and to strike a spark within your heart to take action. The bottom line is that we have been fed lies to accept a pattern of belief that is contrary to God's will and to His divine protection. Furthermore, our sons and daughters are being taught to suck up the lies and join the mainstream by these forces well entrenched within our educational system, political circles, and corporate America. To complicate this further, there are many men and women of faith who are also guilty for not teaching and demonstrating a strong moral belief system to their children. Yet this is our number one responsibility as parents to set a strong foundation for our children. In doing so, they are unknowingly contributing to the problem.

As in the days of Rosa Parks, when she refused to give up her bus seat to a white man and was subsequently arrested for what she believed was injustice, we as people of faith need to take a similar stand or be carried away by the very inaction that is resulting in propagation of iniquity throughout our land. Within Rosa's heart and soul, she understood that we are all human beings made in the image of God. And with that, we all have the very same inalienable rights to protect and embrace that which is good, moral, and godly and to shun that which is evil.

Parks took a stand against a public and national policy that was wrong. Likewise, we, as people of faith, need to take a stand to return God to His throne within our country. The 1947 doctrine of separation of church and state needs to be challenged in terms of its constitutionality and must be overturned. If all of the people of faith within this country would unite under this banner, we could reverse the course of this nation from that of inevitable destruction to that of repentance and redemption. By removing God from our society, we embraced a new master in 1947. Unfortunately, that new master is Satan. If you are reading this for the first time, you may conclude that this is an oversimplified state-ment. However, the 1947 ruling became the new precedent by which all other future rulings against our religious freedoms were based. From a biblical standpoint, we are servants to one of two masters. By turning our back on God, our nation is embracing a new master who is systematically destroying this country and its people. Therefore, it should be a primary goal of the churches of believers to turn this around.

An example of how to get God back into our country is taken from our own history. During the early 1900s, there were two prohibition amendments to the US Constitution that served as a template for legal precedent. We need to look to these as examples to restore "one nation under God." The Eighteenth Amendment to the Constitution was rati-fied during the early 1900s and prohibited the manufacture, sale, and distribution of alcohol within this country. The Eighteenth Amendment to the Constitution was proposed to several state legislatures by the Sixty-Fifth Congress on the 18th of December, 1917, and was declared in a proclamation by the Secretary of State on January 29, 1919, to have been ratified by the legislatures of thirty-six of the forty-eight states. Ratification was completed on January 16, 1919. [mmm]

In fourteen short years, the Twenty-Second Amendment to the Constitution repealed the Eighteenth Amendment and once again permitted the sale and distribution of alcohol in the United States. Section 1 stated that "The eighteenth article of amendment to the Constitution of the United States is hereby repealed." The Twenty-First amendment to the Constitution was proposed to several states by the Seventy-Second Congress on February 20, 1933. In a declaration by the Secretary of State on December 5, 1933, it was ratified by thirty-six of the forty-eight states.

During the early 1900s, this country repealed prohibition for a number of reasons that included economics, enforcement costs, etc. However, the bottom line is that alcohol was once prohibited and then reinstated within this country by amending the Constitution twice—once for and once in repeal.

If we, as people of faith, were determined to take a stand against the greatest injustice and betrayal to our Lord and Savior, we could overturn the Supreme Court ruling of 1947 and the subsequent ruling of 1962 that further denied our children the right to worship their God within our schools.

This should be our charge and banner as faithful, united churches of believers determined to take a stand for God. In the days of Jesus, Israel was occupied by the Roman Empire. During that time, men and women of faith were commanded by God to pray for these leaders and to respect authority. They had neither the power nor the influence to change the legal realms of the ruling government at that time. The bottom line is that they had no choice but to pray for their leaders. In our country, it is quite different.

Men and women of faith within this country have the ability and responsibility to elect and/or influence the election of our leaders. Additionally, we will be held accountable to the decisions we have made in our choices—all of our choices. Today, we outnumber our oppressors by a significant margin. We also have the ability to remove those leaders who are part of the problem, while replacing them with God-fearing men and women—irrespective of political party. This is not a call to violence by any means. It is a call for unity and determination of purpose on a large scale. Therefore:

1. We must continue to pray for our existing leaders and for new candidates who are God-fearing to gain positions of leadership within our government
2. We must support Christian candidates aspiring to become our future leaders
3. We must educate ourselves about our existing incumbents and their core beliefs while determining within ourselves to vote only for those who have a biblical world view, who support God's principles of morality, and who will support the return of "one nation under God" by the overturning of the Supreme Court ruling of 1947
4. We must be very vocal and active in promoting our core beliefs for the kingdom of God without fear of reprisal
5. We must reject and challenge all aspects of evolution and evolutionary theory. As mentioned earlier in this book, evolution is a religion within the scientific community based upon scanty evidence, doctored research, and extreme bias. Any molecular biologist worth his weight in salt knows that evolutionary theory is a charade—yet it is being taught within our schools. Any politician that considers this acceptable and denies intelligent design must be rejected at the polling booth and from future consideration in any leadership appointment
6. We must get involved on a number of fronts to turn this country around.

Getting Involved
and Next Steps

Now is the time for the faithful to take action to defend the moral principals of God within our society. It is very important that you know without a doubt that I do not condone violence. That is not what I am advocating in this chapter or in this book. However, I do believe passionately that this is a critical time in our history when we need to unite under a common banner to reestablish "one nation under God."

The following pages will provide you with insight and guidance on how we can come together as a united church of believers to take back our country. To be successful, we first need to be prepared. We must put on the full armor of God with a determination to march forward into battle.

> **Be prepared.** You're up against far more than you can handle on your own. Take all the help you can get, every weapon God has issued, so that when it's all over but the shouting you'll still be on your feet. Truth, righteousness, peace, faith, and salvation are more than words. Learn how to apply them. You'll

> need them throughout your life. God's Word
> is an indispensable weapon. In the same way,
> prayer is essential in this ongoing warfare.
> Pray hard and long. Pray for your brothers
> and sisters. Keep your eyes open. Keep each
> other's spirits up so that no one falls behind
> or drops out.
>
> Ephesians 6:13 (MSG)

First and foremost, taking a stand is not for the faint of heart. If you choose to take a stand for the kingdom of God, you will need to be grounded in prayer and God's Word. It is critical that you are rooted in the Bible and that you rely upon the Holy Spirit for guidance and strength. Once you have determined to take a stand for God, you will be opening yourself up to attack by the devil and his demons. Furthermore, once you begin moving forward in battle, Satan will put doubt in your mind and will cause all kind of roadblocks to pop up in front of you with the hope that you will give up. When these seasons of doubt and persecution appear, take heart, for you are on the right track, and the enemy is in reaction mode.

I am telling you this at the very beginning of your journey because there are many in this country that are rooted in darkness and will resist you every step of the way. Planning for this in advance will allow you to anticipate and prepare for the battle ahead.

We also need a battle plan that is real, tangible and executable toward tearing down the strongholds of the devil within this country. Within the military, an offensive strategy is adopted to attack the "centers of gravity" (CoG) of the enemy. The premise is to prioritize the attack against the enemy's command and control, highly valued weapon systems, manufacturing assets, bridges, infrastructure, and foot soldiers.

Within this battle, the following CoG's have the most impact toward redeeming this country. They include:

1. Political centers of gravity
2. Legal centers of gravity
3. Educational centers of gravity

Attacking the enemies of God on these fronts will have the most impact toward the faithful gaining control over the sinful policies of this country. With that said, one of the most powerful weapons that Christians have at our disposal is God's truth. This is one weapon that must be used purposefully, strategically, and generously.

> For the **fruit of the light** consists in all **goodness, righteousness and truth.**
> Ephesians 5:9 (NIV)

The truth I speak of, when properly applied, is like a smart bomb that will penetrate deep into the enemy's headquarters while delivering those held hostage into God's light.

> Then you **will know the truth**, and **the truth will set you free.**
> John 8:32 (NIV)

So, what then are the next steps? The following pages will detail what you can do to make a difference. It is up to you if you will take this call to action, to make a difference and be part of the solution. Otherwise, you will continue to go through life complaining as the enemies of God gain further control over this country. If you pick the latter, you will only have yourself to blame as your religious freedoms are further suppressed by public policy, the ACLU, liberal judges, the secular humanist, and spineless politicians.

If you are tired of waiting on the sidelines while your team is getting beaten, then there are a number of actions within this section you can take to make a difference. It is my prayer that you will heed this call to action seriously by taking a stand for the kingdom of God.

> For zeal for your house has eaten me up, and the reproaches and insults of those who reproach and insult you have fallen upon me.
> Psalm 69:9 (Amplified Bible)

The Political Center of Gravity

The political landscape is a hot issue for most Americans and a religious taboo when it comes to endorsing any particular candidate. The churches have been suppressed and outright silenced when it comes to endorsing a God-fearing candidate over one whose policies and personal views are diametrically opposed to the teachings of God. Sadly, the majority of churches stay silent in fear of potentially losing their not-for-profit status for publicly endorsing a political candidate instead of honoring God's Word by protecting and feeding their sheep.

The bottom line is if you consider yourself to be part of the body of Christ, you are commanded by God to make decisions that align with his moral teachings. Ultimately, you will be judged according to your conduct and actions.

> I the LORD have spoken. The time has come for me to act. I will not hold back. I will not have pity, nor will I relent. **You will be judged according to your conduct and your actions, declares the Sovereign LORD.**
> Ezekiel 24:14 (NIV)

Therefore, if a political candidate or incumbent endorses alternative lifestyles, abortion, separation of church and state according to the 1947 Supreme Court ruling, evolution, and any other policy that is contrary to God's Word, **you simply do not vote for or support that candidate**. This has nothing to do with taking a Democratic or Republican position. It has everything to do with taking a godly stand—even when you question the end result.

The concept is simple. If all the Judeo-Christian community of believers were to vote for candidates that supported a biblical view of governance, we would be removing leaders that are of the secular mindset from office. If our leaders were biblically-conscious and applied Christian teachings within their elected positions, they would create and support laws that would enhance the moral fabric of our country. They would also appoint and affirm judges with the same moral standards. If the entire Judeo-Christian community was to embrace this tactic, this country's leadership would be centered solidly on biblical foundation within eight years.

The current division within this country and the churches is exacerbated by the political parties currently in power and their self-serving actions and interests. As a nation, politicians have strayed away from selecting a position that is "for the people" to selecting a position that "protects the party at all costs," even when doing so would result in emboldening our enemies currently engaged in battle with our troops or endorsing policies that subject the citizens of this nation to undue risk. This is unacceptable to the Judeo-Christian community and must be opposed by all the faithful through public protest, the support of godly candidates, and voting at the polls.

A liberal candidate for office who has no regard for God in his or her actions (for most will proclaim a form of godliness in their words) and voting record should never be supported by any person of faith. Such candidates are part of the problem, not part of the solution. You will know who they are, for they are the ones lashing out across party lines in verbal attacks upon a person's character and integrity, when in reality they are the ones in need of close moral and ethical scrutiny.

You may be wondering how you can identify who you support for political office. I will give you one example to show how you can weed out the good from the bad. On June 7, 2006, the Senate was tasked to vote for a constitutional amendment to define marriage as a union between a man and a woman. The reason for this was to protect the states from liberal judges who have taken it upon themselves to enact laws against the will of the people, as was done in Massachusetts.

The argument by those opposing the constitutional amendment was that it was up to the states, which already have laws on books protecting the sanctity of marriage. However, a precedent was already set in Massachusetts and could easily be repeated within every other state throughout this country by liberal judges who have a warped view of what is considered constitutional.

The following is a list of senators that voted against this proposed constitutional amendment to protect the sanctity of marriage. Men and women of faith need to send a strong message to all political parties by not voting for these individuals in the future. Furthermore, we need to align and support any godly candidate that challenges these incumbents when they seek reelection. These senators include:

Akaka (D-HI)	Feinstein (D-GA)	Menendez (D-NJ)
Baucus (D-MT)	Gregg (R-NH)	Mikuiski (D-MD)
Bayh (D-IN)	Harkin (D-IA)	Murray (D-WA)
Biden (D-DE)	Inouye (D-HI)	Nelson (D-FL)
Bingaman (D-NM)	Jeffords (I-VT)	Obama (D-IL)

Boxer (D-CA)	Johnson (D-SD)	Pryor (D-AR)
Cantwell (D-WA)	Kennedy (D-MA)	Reed (D-RI)
Carper (D-DE)	Kerry (D-MA)	Reid (D-NV)
Chafee (R-RI)	Kohl (D-WI)	Salazar (D-CO)
Clinton (D-NY)	Landrieu (D-NJ)	Sarbanes (D-MD)
Collins (R-ME)	Lautenberg (D-NJ)	Schumer (D-NY)
Conrad (D-ND)	Leahy (D-VT)	Snowe (R-ME)
Dayton (D-MD)	Levin (D-MI)	Specter (R-PA)
Dorgan (D-ND)	Lieberman (D-CT)	Stabenow (D-MI)
Durbin (D-IL)	Lincoln (D-AR)	Sununu (R-NH)
Feingold (D-WI)	McCain (R-AZ)	Wyden (D-OR)

Although we may have lost a battle to protect the sanctity of marriage on June 7, 2006, we now have identified those senators who are part of the problem. The senators mentioned above need to be rejected by all people of faith from future political leadership roles within this country. You can rationalize all you want about a political viewpoint or candidate in terms of relative goodness. Irrespective of the emotion supporting a popular candidate, **if any person promotes a policy that is contrary to the moral teachings of God, then that person must not be in a position of leadership**.

In addition, the faithful need to take action in mass when a politician promotes or takes a position that is threatening to our religious freedoms. This protest needs to be very vocal, but must be kept within the limitation of our governing laws. Protests, petitions, marches, bulk calls, and political lobbying are all acceptable.

Lastly, we need to get politically involved. People of faith need to be the ones that are running for political office as mayors, congressmen and congresswomen, legislators, and senators. We must pray continuously for God to raise capable and godly men and women to serve in political leadership positions. We need to be fully engaged while asking God where we would best fit to put Him back on the throne within our country. The Lord may be asking you to serve on the school committee, or you might be inspired by the Holy Spirit to be the next senator, or you may be asked to support a godly candidate. In any case, you need to be plugged into either supporting a God-fearing candidate or choosing to be such a candidate yourself.

The Legal Center of Gravity

This country is governed by laws, many of which have been successfully reshaped by the ACLU and the secular humanists as they align with liberal judges to turn this country from a moral to an amoral society. We need to use litigation as a vehicle for taking a stand against the workers and promoters of iniquity. We need to engage in litigation by taking the legal path against past and present policies that have repressed and censored our freedom of religious expression. En masse, we need to litigate or protest so that our unified actions reverberate from the lower courts all the way up to the United States Supreme Court.

Our enemies take no thought about commencing law suits intended to push God out of our society. As mentioned earlier, the ACLU engages in about six thousand cases every year. Therefore, we must take similar actions to put our enemies on the defense, while establishing momentum to turn the laws back toward supporting our core beliefs. The following is a list of recommended topics prime for individual and class action litigation. They include:

1. **Litigate to repeal the separation of church and state ruling of 1947:** As previously mentioned,

a precedent was set to overturn prohibition back in the early 1900s. That is the basis by which we can justify our overturning of the 1947 separation of church and state ruling. The legal minds within this country need to assemble with a battle cry that mandates the reversal of this unlawful decree and unconstitutional ruling that has led to the decay of the moral center of this country. This must be challenged en masse and must be a major priority for getting the Lord back on the throne within this country.

2. **We need to litigate to overturn the 1962 Supreme Court ruling that kicked God out of our schools.** As Christians, we need to not only put God back on the throne within our country, but also allow our children to connect with their Creator without censorship. I am not advocating forced Bible readings in school. But a child that desires to give thanks to God or to pray or to assemble in a private Bible study on school grounds should not be denied. Additionally, we need to be very aggressive towards allowing any other deviant form of education from permeating the minds of our children.

3. **Litigate to remove any reference to Satan, horoscopes, black magic, and all other occult references from our schools:** It is certainly ironic that God is forbidden within our schools, but Satan is allowed. For example, the mascot of the Chelsea High School in Chelsea, Massachusetts is the "Red Devil." The last time I checked, Satanism is a religion. The same is true with a horoscope, which is in essence the worshipping of the celestial bodies,

stars, and idols. There are public colleges that teach forms of mysticism, which should be litigated. The bottom line is that if all other forms of religious expression are allowed and taught within the public education system, then so, too, should our Judeo-Christian beliefs be given equal consideration and funding support.

4. **Litigate against the educational system to remove evolution from the curriculum and from public grants.** Based upon a small sampling of the evidence against evolution within this book, it is apparent that a believer of evolution needs more faith to accept that theory than one would need in accepting that God created the universe and the world in which we live. Therefore, evolutionary theory is in reality nothing more than a belief system to those who accept its nonsense. This should be litigated at the highest level. Furthermore, all public funds and grants for evolutionary research must cease and desist immediately. If, on the other hand, evolutionary theory is to maintain its place within our school system, then creative design must be included as well. "Equal time," as the liberals call it, would include the same support structure.

5. **Litigate against colleges and high schools for teaching alternative lifestyles:** The constitutionality of having to accept alternative lifestyles within the public venue must be challenged in court.

Under the guise of tolerance and anti-bigotry, our children are being led to believe in and accept a lifestyle that is contrary to the teaching of the Bible. Homosexuality is not an acceptable lifestyle to those professing their belief in Jesus and the Bible. In the same way that adultery, fornication, child molestation, stealing, and murder are condemned in the Bible, so is homosexuality. Therefore, it must not be embraced as an acceptable norm.

The Bible is very clear about sinners, irrespective of the sin. We are to love them, but hate their sinful practices. Jesus died for the sinner, so by the very nature and teachings of the Bible, we are already commanded to love the homosexual as well. The big difference is that we do not accept the sin, nor will we tolerate the teaching of this sinful lifestyle to our children as an acceptable norm.

6. **Litigate against the porn industry, cable and satellite TV companies, hotel chains, adult stores, etc:** Individual and class action lawsuits must be commenced against these organizations that promote sexual deviancy and contribute to all forms of "sexual addiction." The litigation should follow the path established in the suits filed against the cigarette companies, which were sued successfully due to the addictive and harmful nature of cigarettes. The organizations referred to above must be held accountable for the garbage they are promoting, which is contributing to the demise of the family relationship and the increase in sexual addiction and crimes.

The churches of believers need to be on the lookout for deviant acts that can be traced back to these industries and public outlets so that they, too, can be included in class action litigation. If, for example, a pedophile commits a heinous crime and there is evidence that he or she was "inspired" by pornographic materials to commit the crime, then the store that sold the material, the porn industry by which it was produced, and the city that permitted the adult store to sell the material should all be sued.

Furthermore, statistical research that can provide credible probability and correlation that links sexual deviancy to sexual addiction and crime should be explored, documented, and used as evidence to support class action litigation against this sick industry.

As you can see from the litigation examples mentioned above, there is a method to this madness. We need to take an offensive stance toward combating these evils within our country. The American Centers of Law and Justice (ACLJ) and other Christian organizations do a wonderful job in defending our religious rights and freedoms and should be supported. However, you will never win a war if you only take a defensive stance. Eventually the enemy will wear you down. To actually gain ground on the enemy, we must be on the offensive, putting the enemies of God on the defensive.

The Educational Center of Gravity

Forbidding a teacher from keeping a Bible on her desk is not preventing the "establishment of religion." Having a Bible on the desk is merely an expression of faith, or it may simply be a comfort to the teacher. For a country that preaches tolerance for the immoral, we have a lot of nerve forcing our educators to refrain from displaying their faith. Banning a Bible from a teacher's desk and barring her from wearing a cross, while permitting immoral and even hostile topics and symbols to exist in the same educational setting under the protection of freedom of speech is unacceptable and must be challenged in court.

Likewise, when a child proclaims, "one nation under God" or prays with his or her friend, it is not establishing a religion. When a valedictorian's speech is censored by the school by having the lights turned off or by cutting off power to the microphone because she tries to acknowledge the importance of Jesus as the guiding force in her success, it is not the establishment of religion. The student is merely making a factual expression of her faith and must be free to do so.[nnn] Any policy or law that restricts its people from connecting with their God in a public setting is the highest form of hypocrisy, censorship, and, according to our Founding Fathers, unpatriotic.

Rosa Parks understood that her freedoms were being violated when she was forbidden free access to a front row seat on a public bus. Likewise, we are also forbidden from exercising our constitutional right of expression within our public schools and colleges. Therefore, we must protest in a manner similar to that of the civil rights movement, which eventually brought about laws that banned racism and restored freedom to African Americans, just as religious freedom must be restored to the Judeo Christian community of believers.

If you are a student, you should proudly take your Bible to school, even if it means suspension. If you are a parent, you should support your child and challenge any resulting disciplinary action with protest and, if necessary, litigation. If you are a teacher, you should challenge the status quo through the legal system. If the teacher's union does not support your action, you should bring a class action lawsuit against them as well.

Whether you are in grade school or college, you need to read and understand the hoaxes of evolution and be prepared to challenge your teachers by not accepting evolutionary theory. You need to be professional and informed when challenging the hoaxes of evolution so as to avoid being labeled an emotional Jesus freak. Uncontrolled, emotional zeal for God is very annoying to all listeners—especially when you don't have your facts together. Additionally, you need to be informed about the "faith of our Founding Fathers."

> But in your hearts set apart Christ as Lord.
> Always be prepared to **give an answer to**
> **everyone** who asks you to give the reason for
> the hope that you have.
>
> 1 Peter 3:15 (NIV)

I strongly recommend every reader to purchase the following audio training CDs from "Moore on Life" (http://www.mooreonlife.com) to educate yourself in the areas of evolutionary hoaxes and the faith of our Founding Fathers so that you are prepared to provide an intelligent response to those within our educational system who are brainwashed into peddling these lies.

I recommend the following CD series:

- The Apes are Still Swinging
- One Nation Under God: The Faith of our Founding Fathers
- Dismantling the DaVinci Code
- The ACLU & U; An Expose' Of The ACLU's Radical Agenda

These four series are excellent for providing you with a basic foundation for retorting and debating teaching that is contrary to your personal beliefs when they are under attack.

Introduction to Service Before Self Foundation

I have established the Service Before Self Foundation (SBSF) exclusively to engage in scholarly research, publishing, educating, and engaging in litigation for the purpose of defending the United States Constitution, our religious rights, and our liberties.

Our Founding Fathers knew that if we abandoned God, we would eventually fall into destruction. We would also be a nation divided and unprotected by God. Well, that is the current state of this country today. To make matters worse, our Constitution is basically being ignored and misinterpreted without any consequence and without an outpouring of protest from the American people—until now.

SBSF actively protests our nation's turning its back on the Constitution that we have sworn to protect and on God, in whom this nation once put its trust. This is the reason that I have established this foundation. I have also established an interim Web site (http://www.ServiceBeforeSelf.com) until a more suitable site can be established.

I am presently looking for leaders and contributors that will support the ongoing operation of this forum. I am interested in able contributors that will donate their time and resources toward making SBSF a formidable presence for tearing down the walls of religious oppression within this country.

SBSF needs your help to educate the masses about the lies that promote evolution and the separation of church and state while holding our government accountable to the Constitution, which it is sworn to defend.

To support or to become a member of SBSF, please visit the Web site and learn how individuals and organizations can actively take a stand in the defense of this great nation.

<u>SBSF needs volunteers in the following areas:</u>

- Web/Database Developers and Hosting Resources
- Content Managers
- Political Activists
- Political Lobbyists
- Constitutional Attorneys
- Senior Council
- Defense Attorneys
- Political Research Professionals

- Fundraisers
- Sponsors and Financial Backers
- Financial and Bookkeeping Experts
- And an army of foot soldiers to support this action group

You can make a difference in putting God back into **"one nation under God!"**

Become a Beacon of Light
in this Dark World

Throughout this book, the focus has been to lift the reader's level of awareness to the current spiritual state of this country while exposing the lies and deviant behaviors that are contributing to its decline. Therefore, it is critical that the reader evaluate how he or she connects with God in accordance with the moral standards that He has set forth. Lastly, and most importantly, are actions that the reader should consider in order to honor God while positively impacting your community and this nation.

Irrespective of your background, you do not have to be a Billy Graham to have a huge impact for the kingdom of God. If the good Lord can transform this sinful, rebellious author, then I am confident that He can do the same for you. When reflecting upon my own life, I consider myself to be the least within the churches of believers. Irrespective of my shortcomings, God is using me in a great way. He can likewise do the same for you.

I learned about salvation when I was sixteen years old. It was during that time when I accepted Jesus as my Lord and Savior. During the two years that followed, there was no real substance to my relationship with God and, as a result, I began to slide back into sin and worldly influences. I was the one to whom the Bible refers as the "seed sown in the thorns."

> Then he told them many things in parables, saying: "A farmer went out to sow his seed. As he was scattering the seed, some fell along the path, and the birds came and ate it up. Some fell on rocky places, where it did not have much soil. It sprang up quickly, because the soil was shallow. But, when the sun came up, the plants were scorched, and they withered, because they had no root. Other seed fell among thorns, which grew up and choked the plants.
>
> Matthew 13:3-7 (NIV)

> **The one who received the seed that fell among the thorns is the man who hears the word, but the worries of this life and the deceitfulness of wealth choke it, making it unfruitful.**
>
> Matthew 13:22(NIV)

From the time I was eighteen up until my fortieth birthday, I lived a life of rebellion against God, my parents, and my family. I basically did anything I wanted as long as it met my needs—most often at the expense of others. I married at twenty-eight and fathered two boys in my early thirties. Unfortunately, I matured in my career at the expense of my family. I was, at best, a part-time husband and father for the first seven years of my children's lives, due primarily to the intense travel requirements of my career.

I celebrated my fortieth birthday alone in a sports bar in Danvers, Massachusetts. My business was near bankruptcy. I was abandoned by my close friends, away from my family, and questioning whether my marriage would last another year. As I began honestly to reflect upon my life, I could not think of a redeeming quality that I possessed. I was, however, able to think of the lives I had hurt, the people I had disappointed, and the series of angry outbursts that resulted in lost friends and ruined relationships. At this point in my life, I was tired, depressed, and very much alone.

As I drove to my parents' home in Saugus from that sports bar, I continued to reflect upon my life. In a defeated, dejected manner, I spoke to God. **"Jesus, please remove this life from me, I don't want to hurt anyone anymore..."** Almost five years later, I now realize that Jesus honored that prayer. At the time I spoke to God, I just wanted to quit, give up, and consider all things lost. I did not know then that God had other plans for me.

With all my faults and weaknesses, the good Lord wanted to use me, as he does you, in a powerful way—not because of our righteousness, but due to his grace. You see, God loves you despite your righteousness or sin. It was that realization that drove me to give up the fruitless life I was living and seek God with an honest heart. That was the moment when I realized that I have nothing to offer the Lord but a sincere heart coupled with a strong desire to make a difference. In my case, God's plan was and has always been to change me from within and to provide me with a life worth living. I just would not let him do so for over twenty-four years.

Today, I am totally convinced that despite how poorly you view yourself, how many times you have sinned, how many times you have failed in life, the life you have been living, and how many people you have personally hurt or disappointed, God loves you and wants to use you in a powerful way for His glory.

> My brothers, if one of you should wander
> from the truth and someone should bring him

back, remember this: Whoever **turns a sinner
from the error of his way** will save him from
death and cover over a multitude of sins.

James 5: 19-20 (NIV)

That is my desire for you. If you are struggling with sin,
then determine within yourself that you will go forward as
you lean on the Father, Son, and Holy Spirit for strength,
power, and direction. It is my prayer that the Holy Spirit
will guide your thoughts and actions according to His will
and that your life will be transformed into one that gives you
hope, victory, and peace of spirit.

It is at this point that you must determine whether you
will honor God or man as you proceed forward in your life.
I promise you if you honor God with a sincere heart desiring
to glorify His name and kingdom, the outpouring of blessings will be beyond your wildest imagination. If your heart is
right, you will not even have to think about the blessings—
they will just happen. In most cases, you will be pleasantly
surprised. In some cases, you will be overwhelmed.

But, seek first the Kingdom of God and His
righteousness, and all these things will be
added to you.

Matthew 6:33
(English Standard Version)

You know, there is saying that, "It is easier to look up
when you're flat on your back." Well, that is exactly where
I was at one point in my life before I decided to do something about it. It is funny how well you can see when there is
nothing blocking your view. It was at that point that I made
peace with God. It was also during that time that I committed
to go to church and read the Bible, irrespective of my motiva-

tion. I was not going to trust in my own abilities and feelings anymore.

From a business perspective, I knew that I could regroup and be successful again, but I did not want to do so at the expense of my family or relationship with God ever again. Therefore, I determined if I was ever going into business again, I would put God first. That commitment was not a mere euphemism. No longer would I serve my own interest, but from that point forward, I would serve the kingdom of God first. Furthermore, I would create an atmosphere that would allow my customers to connect with God—even if it was only for a few minutes. My mission was to plant seeds of truth about the kingdom of God while exposing the lies that result only in bondage and disappointment to those in sin. Irrespective of political correctness, the world would know by sight and by action that this business was Christian owned and operated. Furthermore, from a secular standpoint, this business would add value to all who enter. The concept was an ordinary automotive service business with a very unique business model.

I decided to create a Christian quick lube, which I named "Trinity Express Lube." It would provide a ten-minute oil change operation similar to the national chains. In December of 2004, I prayed that God would find me a piece of commercial property upon which he would want me to establish this business. The Lord directed me to a location on Valley Avenue in Winchester, Virginia—which was not the most desirable location for this type of business. Yet this is exactly where the good Lord wanted it to be.

If you know anything about the quick lube industry, the location selected had more reasons to fail than to succeed. The city set-back from the road was seventy-five feet, which resulted in the business being blocked from public view by a residential home on one side and a Goodyear operation on the other. I had five competing oil change businesses within a two-mile radius of my location. I was not able to hide my queue based on city directives. The phrase "hiding the queue" refers to a traffic flow design in which cars are directed in back of a building to open bays and then exit through the front of the building. This is so that potential customers approaching from the street are not discouraged from entering the business by viewing long lines at the front of the building. The long lines are hidden in the rear. We were mandated to queue to the front of the building while exiting the back ally road that I had to create at a cost of an additional sixty thousand dollars. Lastly, I was told if I created a Christian quick lube, I would alienate myself from nonbelievers.

When a consulting company evaluated the property and my business model, it strongly recommended that I not establish a quick lube oil change business at that location. Yet the Holy Spirit was steadfast in telling me to stay the course. I kept hearing within my heart that I should "honor God and not the wisdom of man." After significant delays and cost overruns during construction, I opened my doors on July 5, 2005. During the morning on opening day, I had the land, building, and business dedicated and anointed with oil by a local pastor to the Lord. I was also determined that the customer waiting room experience would create an atmosphere that would be inviting to all, but would convey a message of truth, light, and hope.

If you visit Trinity Express Lube today, you will find Bibles, tracks, Scriptures on the walls, books, free Christian CDs, and an iPod playing contemporary Christian songs. Since I have a captive audience in each car owner for ten minutes, my mission is to plant as many seeds as I can within his or her heart for the kingdom of God. This is my ministry. I am a seed planter, and the Holy Spirit is the cultivator of that seed.

As I write the final section of this book, I will be coming up to my first anniversary in a few days. This past year, I have given away over two thousand Christian CDs on God's truth, hundreds of tracks, and Bibles. On numerous occasions, I have prayed with patrons who were going through a tough time in their lives. In return, God has blessed this business beyond my wildest dreams. Most quick lubes will lose money for the first eighteen months of operation, with the majority selling fewer than eight thousand gallons of oil during their first year. Trinity Express Lube turned a profit in its third month of operation and will final out this first year with more than eighteen thousand gallons of oil sold—all this in a location that should not succeed by all human standards of business wisdom.

There is a great lesson to be learned about this business that all should reflect upon within their own lives. It is my hope that you would own these truths and apply them to yourself in an effort to make a difference in this hell-bent world.

These lessons are:

1. Whatever you do in this life, put God at the front line of your business, work, family, ambitions, and everything you do. It may not be politically correct, it may seem radical, it may be evaluated by those around you as out of the mainstream, and you may even be persecuted for your stand—but by doing so, you will be lifting God up, and you will be blessed. If you come to Trinity Express Lube, you will have no doubt that it is a Christian-operated business. I am proud of my God. He is front and center in my business. Likewise, if you take a stand in business, politics, activism, or litigation to defend our Constitution and religious freedoms, place God at the center of your plans.

I am not ashamed of the Gospel, because it is
the power of God for the salvation of everyone
who believes.

Romans 1:16 (NIV)

2. When you decide to take a stand for God, you will
   go through trials that will hinder your efforts each
   step of the way. I had nothing but problems stemming from the site plan that I had to accept from
   the city, which was anathema to the success of this
   type of business. I incurred enormous expense in
   clearing the land, which required that I break up
   and remove approximately fifty truck loads of rock
   from the site. I experienced excessive construction
   delays and cost overruns.

As I mentioned before, if you decide to take a stand for
God, you, too, will be attacked and hindered each step of
the way. It is not a question of whether you will be attacked,
but when, by whom, and how. If you take a political stand
for God, you will be labeled a bigot, a zealot, a homophobe,
and a right-wing extremist. Those throughout history that
have made a stand for God were persecuted in one way or
another—including Jesus. You will be no different.

3. If you keep God at the front, the trials and persecu-
   tions bent on defeating your efforts will prove to
   be a blessing in disguise. I am convinced that all of
   the setbacks and issues with this site occurred so
   God could truly demonstrate His glory by enabling
   me to overcome these obstacles to my ultimate
   success—which was far greater than I had even
   planned. Think about it. If I had had the perfect
   location, site plan, demographics, limited compe-
   tition, and so forth, how could I claim that God

blessed this operation? People would just come to the conclusion that I did well because of the location. However, God has turned these notable obstacles into a testimony of His power and glory by growing my business by more than two times the national average in its first year.

If you ask God to use you for His glory, you may find yourself working in a role that seems to be making no headway. You may say to yourself, "Why should I bother proceeding when I'm not really making much of a difference?" The reality is that you may be making a significant impact, but you just don't know it yet.

In the past year, I have given thousands of Christian materials away to expose the lies of the "separation of church and state," "evolution," "debunking the DaVinci Code," and "the ACLU." Sometimes it is easy to question whether all of these giveaways are making any difference at all. But that is not my job. My ministry is to plant seeds of truth. It is up to the Holy Spirit and the providence of God to plant the seeds in good soil. You never know—these materials may end up in the hands of a constitution law attorney who becomes inspired by the Holy Spirit to make a difference. The bottom line is to not give up and let God be God.

4. All successes are from God and not from your own ability. As I reflect today on the success of Trinity Express Lube, I find it amusing that, instead of hearing all of the reasons why this business should fail, I am now hearing praise regarding my excellent business skills. My response is always the same: "God has blessed this business according to His glory. I had nothing to do with it—with the exception of being obedient."

In the same way, if you take a stand for God and the results of your efforts bring forth success, never forget the catalyst behind the achievement—God. Once you loose that perspective, pride will set in, and Satan will have a foothold on your life. Eventually, you will fail as you shift from leaning on God to leaning on your own capabilities.

What On Earth Does Trinity Express Lube Have to Do with Changing the Direction of this Sinful Country?

Plenty. Trinity Express Lube is a model example of honoring God in everything you do. If you own a business, use it to glorify God. If you don't, support one that does. Make it a point to pick up the *Shepherd's Guide*, which is a yellow pages of Christian businesses, and provide those businesses with your support. Take a stand, support a cause, make a difference, craft your life in a manner that puts Jesus front and center at home and in your business. Make it your mission to be a light in this dark world.

> No one lights a lamp and hides it in a jar or puts it under a bed. Instead, **he puts it on a stand, so that those who come in can see the light.**
>
> Luke 8:16 (NIV)

Therefore, apply your God-given talents toward edifying the churches of believers while providing a light of truth to the unsaved and lost. Keep in mind that light does three things:

1) It provides a beacon of hope to those who are lost
2) It chases out the darkness—a very small light can illuminate a large, dark room

3) Unfortunately, it also lets the enemy know that you are there. Therefore, being prepared for battle in advance is critical.

If you know of companies that support organizations that are contrary to the moral teachings of God, don't purchase their goods and services. For example, Progressive Insurance has donated millions to the ACLU. The Ford Motor Company supports the gay agenda. In both cases, people of faith should not support these organizations. I have bought Ford automobiles for years and presently own two of them, but will not purchase another one until Ford changes its corporate policies regarding alternative lifestyles. This is not bigotry. It is taking a moral stand in an amoral world. Most people would not support a company that had a corporate policy that supported adultery. Neither should the churches of believers support any business that promotes homosexuality.

In closing, only you can make a difference. As this country continues down the path toward God's judgment, there are some Christians who are content in living their lives on the religious sidelines, totally separated from those in need. Jesus did not take this approach. Throughout the Gospels, Jesus went to the lost, healed the sick, and drove demons out of those in bondage.

Likewise, organize yourself for battle against those who suppress our religious freedoms and expose them to the light of truth.

It is only then that will we be able to turn back the tide of religious intolerance to a nation grounded in the principles of God. The Christian community has been taking a beating since the inception of the ACLU and turning our back on God in the 1947 Supreme Court ruling. It is now time for us to fight back...

But, as for me, I watch in hope for the LORD, I wait for God my Savior; my God will hear me. Do not gloat over me, my enemy! Though I have fallen, I will rise. Though I sit in darkness, the LORD will be my light. Because I have sinned against him, I will bear the LORD's wrath, until he pleads my case and establishes my right. He will bring me out into the light; I will see his righteousness.

Micah 7:7-9 (NIV)

Appendix A

For those who have just accepted Jesus Christ as their Lord and Savior, it is critical that the seed of His salvation take root and be nourished in the truth of God's Word. You need to know your Savior and to understand His will for you. The following are some helpful next steps that you should consider before taking any actions within this book. The apostle Paul went into the desert for a few years to know God before venturing out in his ministry. Similarly, an athlete prepares him or herself before competing in sports to avoid the risk of injury and be effective in the game. I suggest the following to prepare yourself as you go forward:

1. Ground yourself in a church that follows biblical teaching with Jesus Christ as its center and has salvation as its primary purpose.

2. Begin reading the Bible, starting with the Gospel of John from the New Testament. John speaks about the love and passion of Jesus and is a must-read for new believers. You should then read the other Gospels of Matthew, Mark, and Luke. From there, begin reading the Acts of the Apostles

through the end of the Bible, stopping short of Revelation. Revelation will only confuse you without an understanding of prior readings and studies from the Old Testament.

3. Before you being each reading, pray to God that the Holy Spirit will provide you with an under-standing of His Word. Doing so will prepare your heart toward receiving God's Word and instruction.

4. Once you have completed your readings, consider purchasing *The One Year Bible*, which will provide you with 365 daily readings that include portions of the Old Testament, the New Testament, the Psalms, and Proverbs. It is an excellent regiment to get through the entire Bible in one year, while not getting bogged down in sections that are hard to traverse, such as the Book of Numbers. You may find this book at http://www.christianbook. com.

5. Make it a personal mission to bring the truth of salvation to your family members. Eternity is as stake here, for we are only going to be alive for a short time on this planet. The Bible describes life as a puff of smoke and a mist, which appears for a short time and then disappears into eternity. Therefore, it is critical that your family under-stands God's plan for salvation in their lives. Be also a living testimony of how God is changing you, so they are not badgered, but are loved into his kingdom. Your job is only to keep planting the seeds of truth until they take root in the good soil of their hearts. It is the job of the Holy Spirit to

convince their hearts. Therefore, keep praying for your family and don't give up.

6. Consider reading *The Purpose Driven Life* by Rick Warren. This is an excellent book that outlines what God's purpose is for you and your life and provides a strong foundation for new believers.

7. Ask the Lord to provide you with the heart of a servant, so that you can be used in a mighty way for His Kingdom and according to His will.

It is my prayer that you will be deeply grounded in the truth of God's Word and that the Holy Spirit will fill your heart and mind in accordance with His will in Jesus' name.

End Notes

a   Revelations, Chapters 7 and 8.

b   Gregory Koukl, "What was the Faith of Our Founding Fathers," http://www.str.org/free/reflections/social_ issues/whatwast.htm

c   The Deist belief is based solely on reason, in a God who created the universe and then abandoned it, assuming no control over life, exerting no influence on natural phenomena, and giving no supernatural revelation.

d   John Eidsmoe, Christianity and the Constitution, (Grand Rapids: Baker, 1987), p. 43.)

e   George Washington, Programs and Papers (Washington: U.S. George Washington Bicentennial Commission, 1932)

f   Policy #92, "Religious Bodies' Tax Exemption"…it states, "The ACLU opposes the tax-exemption of all churches…"

g   US Constitution: Amendments, "Article 1", U.S. Library of Congress

h   Preamble of the U.S. Constitution

i   Faith of Our Founding Fathers, Tim LaHaye; 1987; pp122

^j Gallard Hunt and James B. Scott, ed., The Debates in the Federal Convention of 1787 Which Framed the Constitution of the United States of America, reported by James Madison (New York: Oxford University Press, 1920), pp. 181-82

^k http://www.aclu.org/about/index.html "About Us" section, November, 2005.

^l "The ACLU vs America – Exposing the Agenda to Redefine Moral Values", by Alan Sears and Craig Osten, 2005, by Alliance Defense Fund; pg 9.

^m Ibid pg. 11 – Cross Reference: George Grant, *Trial and Error: The American Civil Liberties Union and Its Impact on Your Family* (Brentwood, TN: Wolgemuth and Hyatt, 1989), 38-39.

ⁿ http//www.nrlc.org/abortion/facts/abortionstat.html

^o A Manhattan-based public-interest law firm is defending NAMBLA in a $200 million civil lawsuit filed by Mr. and Mrs. Robert Curley. The Curleys claim that Charles Jaynes was driven by the literature and website of NAMBLA, an outfit that advocates sex between grown men and little boys that resulted in the brutal death of their ten-year-old son, Jeffrey.

^p ACLU Policies: 2a, 4d, 4g, 4e and 211

^q Sears & Olsen Pg47; Reference: Debra Saunders, "One Man's Animal Husbandry," Creators Syndicate, March 21, 2001

^r "ACLU Defends Library against Parents Seeking Internet Censorship," ACLU Press Release, June 1998

^s "Ban on Gays in the Military Goes on Trial: "Don't Ask, Don't Tell,' Faces Challenge in Brooklyn," ACLU press release, March 12, 1995; http://archive.aclu.org/news/n031295c.html.

^t "1992 Policy Guide of the ACLU," policy 62a, p. 120, and policy 86, p. 168.

[u]   Michael Denton: "Evolution: A Theory in Crisis," Adler and Adler, Publishers, Inc. 1996

[v]   Monod, J. (1972) Chance and Necessity, Collins, London, p134

[w]   The History of the Universe - Summary of Cosmology and Dark Energy, Morgan Wascko, Louisiana State University, MiniBoone Experiment.

[x]   Emile Borel, Probabilities and Life, Dover 1962, chapters 1-3

[y]   Virtual Fossil Museum: http://www.fossilmuseum.net/Paleobiology/CambrianExplosion.htm

[z]   Samuel Paul Welles, "Paleontology", World Book Encyclopedia, vol. 15 (1978): p. 85.

[aa]   Creation Defense, "Evidence Against Evolution", by Nicholas Comninellis, M.D.; 2001 by Master Books

[bb]   R.E. Walsh and R.S. Crowell, editors, Proceedings of the First International Conference on Creationism, "Mount St. Helens and Catastrophism," by S.A. Austin (Pittsburgh, PA: Creation Science Fellowship, 1986)

[cc]   F.A. Barnes, "Mine Operation Uncovers Puzzling Remains of Ancient Man," Times Independent, Moab, Utah, June 3, 1971.

[dd]   Wayne Jackson, Creation, Evolution, and the Age of the Earth (Stockton, CA: Courier Publications, 1989), p.13

[ee]   Wakefield Dort Jr., "Mummified Seals of Southern Victoria Land," Antarctica Journal, Washington, vol. 6 (September—October 1971): p. 211.

[ff]   Alan C. Riggs, "Major Carbon – 14 Deficiency in Modern Snail Shells from Southern Nevada Springs," Science, vol. 224 (April 6, 1984); p58.

[gg]   S.A. Austin, "Excess Argon within Mineral Concentrates from the New Dacite Lava Dome at Mount St. Helen Volcano," CEN Technical Journal, 10 (3):335-343 (1986).

hh Encyclopedia Britannica Online;

ii Walt Brown, *In the Beginning: Compelling Evidence for Creation and the Flood,* (6th rev. ed.: Center for Scientific Creation, 5612 N. 20th Place, Phoenix, AZ 85016, U.S.A.; 1995;230 pp.;

jj J.W.G. Johnson, *The Crumbling Theory of Evolution* (3d printing, Los Angeles: Perpetual Eucharistic Adoration, Inc., P.O. Box 84595, Los Angeles, CA 90073, U.S.A., 1987), p. 40.

kk Johnson, op. cit., pp. 37-39. See also "The Piltdown Hoax - Further Revelations," in Bowden, op. cit., pp. 177-194.

ll Patrick O'Connell, Science of Today and the Problems of Genesis_, p. 115.

mm Alan Guttmacher Institute, the research arm of Planned Parenthood;   http://www.abortionno.org/Resources/fastfacts.html

nn Angelo, E.J., "Psychiatric Sequelae of Abortion: The Many Faces of Post-Abortion Grief" Linacre Quarterly, 59(2): 69-80, 1992; Brown, D., Elkins, T.E., Lardson, D.B., 'Prolonged Grieving After Abortion,' J Clinical Ethics, 4(2):118-123

oo Breast cancer: the protective effect of pregnancy, Medina D; Department of Molecular and Cellular Biology, Baylor College of Medicine, Houston, Texas, USA.

pp "Long-Term Physical & Psychological Health Consequences of Induced Abortion: Review of the Evidence," by J.M. Thorp, Jr., MD, K.E. Hartmann, MD, PhD, and E.M. Shadigian, MD. OB/GYN Survey 58(1): 67-79, 2003.

qq "The outcome of pregnancy after threatened abortion", Hertz JB, Heisterberg L.; PMID: 3984691 [PubMed - indexed for MEDLINE]

rr Online Definition: http://www.drugs.com/CG/PLACENTA_PREVIA.html

ss William Donohue, *The Politics of the American Civil Liberties Union* (New Brunswick, NJ: Transaction Press, 1990), 102. excerpt from: Alan Sears and Graig Osten: *The ACLU vs. America*; Broadman & Holman Publishers, 2005

tt http://www.discoverthenetworks.org

uu Hebrews 2:2 (NIV)

vv http://www.familysafemedia.com/pornography_statistics.html

ww Time Reported (December 20, 1999 Vol. 154 no. 25

xx Dr. Victor B. Cline, "Pornography's Effect on Adults and Children."

yy http://www.familysafemedia.com/pornography_statistics.html

zz Christian evangelical ministry dedicated to uniting men to become "godly influences" in the world

aaa Mathew 15:14.

bbb Enrique T. Rueda, The Homosexual Network (Old Greenwich, Connecticut: The Devin Adair Company, 1982), p. 201

ccc http://www.aspeneducation.com/factsheetpromiscuity.html

ddd Source, Centers for Disease Control, Atlanta, GA

eee "ACLU battles 'abstinence-only' education", 2005 WorldNetDaily.com, Sep 22, 2005

fff "Life Application Bible Commentary: Romans", Bruce Barton, David Veerman Neil Wilson; Tyndale House Publishers, Inc. 1992, P129.

ggg John 10:10 (NIV)

hhh The Bible Knowledge Commentary; John F. Walvaued & Roy B. Zuck; Sources: Encyclopedia Britannica, under the word "Egypt"; Lionel Casson, Ancient Egypt (New York: Time-Life Books, 1965); Pier Montet,

Egypt and the Bible (Philadelphia: Fortress Press, 1968).

[iii] http://www.theconservativevoice.com/articles/article.html?id=8986

[jjj] Minister Joe Wright, Central Christian Church, 2900 North Road, Wichita, KS 67226 ; 1996

[kkk] Isaiah 5:20

[lll] In 1955, Rosa Parks refused to give her bus seat to a white man. She was arrested for her defiance.

[mmm] See *Dillon v. Gloss*, 256 U.S. 368, 376 (1921).

[nnn] http://www.aclj.org/trialnotebook/read.aspx?id=371